A Guide to the
Salem Witchcraft Hysteria
of 1692

A GUIDE TO THE
Salem Witchcraft Hysteria
OF 1692

David C. Brown

Photographs by the Author

The frontispiece is a detail of an engraving taken from John W. Barber's *Historical Collections*, published in Worcester in 1839. The view is from the intersection of Washington and Front Streets in Salem, looking north on Washington Street. The building in the middle of the street is the old Essex County Courthouse. It stood a short distance north of the site of the 1692 courthouse in which the Salem witchcraft trials were held. The building with pilasters on the right is City Hall, built in 1837 and still standing today.

Copyright © 1984, David C. Brown
Second printing, 1988
Third printing, 1991
Fourth printing, 1994
Fifth printing, 1997
Library of Congress Card Number 84-164658
ISBN 0-9613415-0-5

To Elizabeth

Contents

Preface

The following work has been written to afford those visiting the Salem environs a means of acquainting themselves with the physical remains of the outbreak of witchcraft in Essex County in 1692. It is not intended to shed fundamentally new light on the events of that year; rather, it should serve to sketch the history of the era and integrate that history with a list of the sites still extant today. Therefore, I feel it necessary to apologize for any omissions or biases which might color this account of the witchcraft. As brevity is desired in any tourguide, many details have been omitted here. They can nevertheless be ferreted out using the bibliographical section which concludes this work. Above all, I have tried to convey the eeriness and mystery of many of the occurrences of the hysteria; that had we been alive in Salem in the seventeenth century, we too would have felt our community the target of an onslaught by Satan and his legions.

This work was born of personal frustration in my attempts to locate the important sites associated with the witchcraft delusion. Not a native of Massachusetts, I felt somewhat obliged to provide a written account for those who, like myself, visit the Salem area infrequently and desire to see the sites of the witchcraft. On my previous visits to Salem I could never locate a thorough and comprehensive guide to the events of 1692. I thus found myself in a position similar to that of the Reverend John Hale, in 1692 the minister of the First Church in Beverly who, in the preface to his account of the witchcraft (*A Modest Enquiry into the Nature of Witchcraft*, pub. 1702) wrote:

> And I have waited five years for some other person to undertake it, who might doe it better than I can, but find none; and judge it better to do what I can, than that such a work should be left undone.

Thus the following tale.

This book is divided into five parts: a history of the Salem witchcraft hysteria; a brief chronology of the witchcraft; a list of the sites pertinent to the witchcraft which can be seen today; a section of maps pinpointing the locations of these sites for the towns of Salem, Danvers, and Beverly; and a selected bibliography for the interested reader. The history, sites, and map sections are all interconnected. Each site has been identified by a number. This number is used consistently in the history, sites, and map sections to refer to that site alone. Illustrations are also numbered and cross-referenced to the sites section. For example, the Rebecca Nurse house in the history section is identified as "(Site 6; Plate 14)." A description of the Nurse house can therefore be found in the sites section under site "6." Its location on the map of Danvers is also listed by that same number, "6." A photograph of the Nurse house can be found by looking up "Plate 14" in the illustrations.

Finally, a word must be said about the quotations in this book which I have chosen not to footnote. All quotations are from either the original court documents of 1692 or are taken from contemporary accounts of the witchcraft. The quotations have been given in their original spellings except in the few cases where the original spellings are nearly unintelligible. Punctuation has also been slightly modernized. Material inserted into quotations by the author to clarify ambiguities has been enclosed in brackets, "[ ]." The author would be happy to provide the source of any quoted material to the interested reader.

David C. Brown
Washington Crossing, Pennsylvania
1984

A Guide to the
Salem Witchcraft Hysteria
of 1692

History

Background

In 1692, the colony of Massachusetts Bay in New England was an isolated foothold in the wilderness of the North American continent, a small light of civilization clinging to the boundaries of the brooding gloom of the unknown western lands. The population was scattered over a vast countryside. Villages and farms were separated by great distances. Communication and travel were exceedingly slow, and the isolation of the people was exacerbated by the constant threat of Indian attacks and the whimsical but devastating forces of nature.

Many of the colony's inhabitants counterbalanced their physical solitude in the New World with a spiritual foundation in the Calvinist doctrines of the Puritans of Mother England. But their spiritual hope proved nearly as bleak as their physical condition. The Puritans postulated an afterlife consisting of either everlasting bliss or eternal torment. The individual believer, however, was incapable of gaining his salvation by virtue of any act he might perform. God had instead predestined those to be saved from damnation. These were the Elect. The rest were consigned to the fires of perdition. The individual had no control over his own fate; it was left solely to the authority of an omnipotent God.

This unquestioning obedience to God's mandates was the hallmark of Puritan society. Every occurrence in men's lives was part of God's overriding plan for the universe. Any good which came into people's lives was the direct result of God's mercy and beneficence; misfortunes, however, were attributed to an entirely different source. God occasionally permitted His fallen angel, Satan, to bring misery to the land as part of God's judgment on the people for deviating from His chosen path. The Puritan world was framed in this juxtaposition of good and evil, in an era before the Age of Reason, when men would begin seeking answers through secular means.

The combined forces of Puritanism and isolation created an environment in which all actions were attributed to mystical powers which governed the world and were ever outside the control of men. The slightest mishap was attributed to some devil who had been unleashed by God to punish the person concerned. The surrounding countryside, it was supposed, abounded with demons poised to snatch the righteous person from the fold of God. Strange diseases, coincidental occurrences, and other miseries were all caused by Satan's servants. With their neighbors far away and unable to give support, people turned to their inner fears when they heard strange noises or imagined strange happenings. To these New England Puritans, the devil's legions roamed almost at will over the land, and their object was to subvert the kingdom of God on earth. Their greatest chance came in 1692 in a wayside community known as Salem Village (now Danvers, Massachusetts).

The spiritual leader of Salem Village in 1692 was the Reverend Samuel Parris. He had started his theological training at Harvard College but took leave before completion and went to work as a merchant in the Barbados, an island in the Caribbean. The business world proved unprofitable for Parris, and in 1689, at the age of thirty-five, he returned to the ministry. Not having completed his schooling at Harvard, he had to settle for a position in the relatively obscure parish of Salem Village, north of Boston. The members of the Village church allowed him use of the parish parsonage (Site 1; Plate 1) as his residence. Upon his arrival there, Parris embarked on a mission to have the parsonage and its accompanying grounds ceded to him in per-

(Plate 1; Site 1)
Foundation of the
1692 Parsonage,
Danvers.

petuity, a request which did not endear him to his parishioners.

Parris had returned to New England from the Caribbean with more than a tarnished regard for his business savvy. He brought with him, besides his immediate family—his wife Elizabeth (Site 9a; Plate 2), his daughter Betty, and niece Abigail Williams—a slave couple, John and Tituba Indian. The duties of the minister and his wife were many. Parris was always busy writing sermons or wrangling with his flock while his wife was often away on errands of mercy in the Village. Thus, while John Indian tended to the parsonage grounds, care of nine-year-old Betty and eleven-year-old Abigail fell to the womanservant Tituba. Tituba was no ordinary household slave. She had been reared in the Barbados, steeped in the voodoo and mystical incantations which were part of the culture of her people. The transition to the bleak ways of the Puritans must have been particularly taxing for Tituba. To while away the tedium and

(Plate 2; Site 9a) Grave of Elizabeth Parris, Danvers.

chores of the winter months of 1691–92, she regaled Betty and Abigail with strange tidings from the Caribbean: of the rites and the magical deeds she had witnessed. She familiarized the two girls, who were eager for a forbidden release from the strictures of Puritanism, with the doings of witches. Through her tales—to the future detriment of Essex County—she furnished the children with knowledge and a working vocabulary of the occult.

The parsonage was the center of life for Salem Village. Many people would come to the parsonage to seek the counsel of Reverend Parris, or they might send a surrogate, a servant or daughter, instead. Apparently, when other young Village women visited the minister's house, they were initiated into Tituba's circle, were told of the slave's Caribbean years, and perhaps shown simple tricks of magic. Tituba, unaware of her tales' repercussions, probably thrived on the increased attention she received from the maids of the area. Slowly the circle of girls expanded.

The first to come were those who lived in the immediate vicinity of the parsonage: Susannah Sheldon and Elizabeth Booth, both eighteen, and seventeen-year-old Mary Walcott. These older girls no doubt confided their secret knowledge of Tituba to their confidantes. Eventually more girls joined the covert group: Elizabeth Hubbard, the seventeen-year-old servant of the Village physician William Griggs; Mary Warren and Sarah Churchill, both twenty; and Mercy Lewis, a nineteen-year-old servant in the household of Sergeant Thomas Putnam, one of the most important Village families. Mercy brought with her Putnam's daughter Ann (Site 11) who, at twelve years of age, would play a pivotal role in the events to follow.

For young Ann had a memory which predated her own twelve years. She was the daughter of Ann Putnam, Sr., a woman who had led a life of misfortune and who believed that her misery was in large part caused by others who disliked her. Ann Putnam, Sr. was set on a course of vengeance in Salem Village. When the time came, she would use her young daughter to exact her revenge. During the ensuing months, many would marvel at young Ann's ability to recall events which had occurred years prior to her birth. Her mind had been filled with the passionate hatred of her mother's bitter memories.

The participants in Tituba's circle were playing with psychological dynamite. They knew full well that their meddlings in the black arts warranted eternal damnation from God. But Tituba's tales and the relief from domestic drudgery which they provided were too enticing. Week after week the girls visited the Barbados slave, and on Sundays sat in the Village meeting while the Reverend Parris thundered fire, brimstone, and damnation. Eventually, the contradiction began to create physical symptoms in the girls themselves.

It began with young Betty Parris sometime in January 1692. Torn between fear for her soul and loyalty to her friends, she told no one about their clandestine meetings with Tituba, but instead began uttering strange sounds, crawling into holes and under chairs, and adopting strange postures with her body. The alarmed Parris household riveted its attention upon her. Abigail

Williams, the niece, on seeing the concern lavished upon little Betty, began mimicking her cousin to gain similar attention. Abigail had none of Betty's sensitivity and frailty. She was a girl who could seize upon opportunities to gain attention and discomfit her elders. Her subsequent behavior indicates that she consciously and maliciously tailored her actions to achieve those ends.

One by one, Tituba's entire circle of girls was beset by the strange behavior which had first affected Abigail and Betty. Essentially, the girls had two choices: expose their dealings with the slave in the magical arts, or follow the trail blazed by the Parris children. They chose, for the moment, the easier path. To have revealed to their parents or masters their secret meetings with Tituba would have brought upon them the censure of the community and accompanying shame. But one cannot live a lie for long without eventually believing it the truth. Slowly the girls' antics, "fitts" as they were called, became ingrained in their behavior. The witchcraft hysteria had begun.

The girls' fits must have been awesome to behold. Reverend Deodat Lawson, who had preceded Samuel Parris as minister at Salem Village and had returned to his former parish to witness these events, said that the motions of the girls' bodies were "so strange as a well person could not Screw their Body into; and as to the violence also it is . . . much beyond the Ordinary force of the same person when they are in their right mind." Reverend John Hale (Site 24; Plate 3 and Site 25; Plate 4), minister of the First Church in Beverly, described the fits in similar terms:

> their arms, necks, and backs turned this way and that way, and returned back again, so as it was impossible for them to do of themselves, and beyond the power of any Epileptick Fits, or natural Disease to effect.

The Reverend Cotton Mather (Site 40b; Plate 5), a Puritan divine of Boston and a prolific writer on the subject of witches, noted that the fits "could not possibly be Dissembled." What then was the cause of this strange behavior? The keenest intellects in all Massachusetts could offer no explanation. But to the

(Plate 3; Site 24) John Hale House, Beverly.

average Puritan mind the girls' behavior meant one thing alone: witchcraft.

Sometime in early February, Parris sought medical advice from Dr. Griggs concerning the girls' maladies. Seventeenth-century medicine was in no state to deal with the disorder which presented itself in Salem Village. There was nothing in medical training which familiarized the doctor with what now confronted him. He took recourse by declaring his fear that the girls were bewitched.

Griggs's diagnosis of the girls' ailment came as little surprise to the inhabitants of the Village. It remained only to determine who was responsible for tormenting the girls. Parris invited two neighboring ministers, John Hale of Beverly and Nicholas Noyes (Site 16d) of Salem Town (modern day Salem), to meet with him at the Village parsonage for prayer and advice. These three men, together with the forces of personal vengeance at work in Essex County, would ultimately provide much of the impetus for the witchcraft accusations to come. Noyes, a fearless Calvinist, would labor incessantly to uproot and destroy the

(Plate 4; Site 25) Grave of Reverend John Hale, Beverly.

abomination of witchcraft once it had been discovered. Parris would prove especially forward in the prosecutions, perhaps to obscure the embarrassing fact that the girls' "fitts" (the group was by now known about the countryside as "the afflicted") had begun in his household. Hale suffered from memories of his crucial role in obtaining the acquittal of a woman charged with witchcraft several years before. Troubled, Hale asked himself if he had been mistaken in defending the accused and, if so, if his error had permitted this new outbreak of evil in 1692. In his second exposure to witchcraft, he was not to prove so merciful.

Dr. Griggs had pronounced the afflicted girls bewitched. Thus responsibility for discovering their tormentors fell by default from the physical to the spiritual authorities in Essex

(Plate 5; Site 40) Tomb of the Mather Family, Boston.

County. If the girls were, indeed, bewitched, then witches who covenanted with the devil instead of with Christ were present somewhere in Massachusetts Bay. The three ministers resolved that the girls be interrogated as to the source of their misery. In the waning days of February 1692 they started a cautious questioning. They began by asking the girls what ailed them and why they behaved so strangely. The ministers' queries elicited no response except further moanings and unintelligible noises. With witchcraft ever in the backs of their minds, the ministers gradually framed their inquiries in a more leading fashion. "Who afflicts you?" they asked. Under relentless probing, the girls finally began to reveal the names of their tormentors.

Just before the girls made their first accusations, however, Tituba resorted to the black arts one last time in an attempt to ferret out the witches herself. On the advice of Mary Sibley, a member of Parris's congregation, the slavewoman tried a traditional test to discover the malefactors. With the help of her husband, John, Tituba baked a witch cake made from rye meal mixed with the urine of the afflicted girls and fed the cake to the household dog. If their aim was to raise the witches who plagued the girls, they got more than they ever bargained for.

Accusations and Examinations

When the girls began to name names, Tituba, their master and teacher, headed the list. Accused with her were two other women, both of ill repute in the Village, Sarah Good (Site 29; Plate 6) and Sarah Osborne. Good was the wife of William Good, a laborer in the Village. William was not the best provider for his family and Sarah often went begging from door to door seeking provisions for her children. She was a pipe-smoking, defiant woman whose unkempt appearance made her look much older than her thirty-eight years. It came as no surprise to anyone that her name was being bandied about as that of a witch. Sarah Osborne, the third of the accused, was bedridden from the infirmities of advanced age. She also had suffered in the past from the malicious gossip of the community. Years before she had permitted her manservant and later husband, Alexander Osborne, to live with her in her house (Site 8; Plate 7), a great impropriety to the scandalmongers of the Village. On

(Plate 6; Site 29) Solart-Woodward House, Wenham.

February 29 warrants for the arrests of Good, Osborne, and Tituba were sworn out by the magistrates of Salem Town, John Hathorne (Site 16a) and Jonathan Corwin (Site 21; Plate 8 and Site 22; Plate 9). The constables were ordered to bring the three women to the ordinary of Nathaniel Ingersoll (Site 2; Plate 10) in Salem Village at ten o'clock on the morning of March 1, the following day. There Hathorne and Corwin would examine them on suspicion of practicing witchcraft on the bodies of the afflicted girls.

Those who would be accused of witchcraft in 1692 would face a two-part legal process. The accused would first be brought before the authorities and examined. If the evidence indicated that the person was a witch, she would be committed to prison and held to await trial. Only upon trial could the accused be convicted. As events developed, most of those examined would later stand trial, the evidence brought against them at examination having almost proved them witches.

The assemblage of the magistrates at Salem Village on Tues-

(Plate 7; Site 8) Sarah Osborne House, Danvers.

day, March 1, caused a great commotion among the people. A large crowd gathered at the ordinary to see the accused and witness their examinations. The interrogation of suspected witches was, after all, far more interesting to the populace than the doldrums of everyday New England life. Indeed, the number of spectators was so large that Ingersoll's inn could not contain them. So the site of the examinations was moved a short distance down the road to the Village meetinghouse (Site 3; Plate 11). There, one after the other, the three women were paraded into the presence of Hathorne, Corwin, and the accusing girls, who fell into terrible fits and convulsions at the sight of their supposed tormentors.

Sarah Good was the first to be brought before the magistrates. When she entered the room, the girls fell to their fits, complaining that Good's specter was moving about the room, pinching and biting them. This was the essence of spectral evidence which was to prove so destructive in the examinations

(Plate 8; Site 21) Jonathan Corwin House, Salem.

and trials to come. A witch supposedly permitted the devil to appear in her image or shape, an entity invisible to the normal, unbewitched eye, to torment her victims. She herself did not have to be physically present with her shape when the torment-ing was done. In this manner, a witch's specter could afflict someone miles away while her physical body could be in an al-together different place. But the witches' specters could not es-cape detection forever. The witch cake affair had "opened" the eyes of the afflicted girls to the specters which afflicted them. With their spectral vision they could see the image of the witch as she practiced her diabolical methods on the innocents.

Good faced the girls' antics and their cries against her with defiance. "What evil spirit have you familiarity with?" Ha-thorne asked her. "None," she replied. She denied having made a contract with the devil or having tormented the "children." Thwarted, Hathorne turned to subtler means to trap the woman. With the girls tumbling about on the floor, crying that Good afflicted them, how could one not believe that she was a witch? "Who doe you imploy then?" to afflict them, he queried. "I im-ploy nobody. I scorn it," came her reply. But even Sarah Good was overcome by the tumult about her. When asked who hurt the girls, she shifted the blame to a fellow defendant. "It was osburn" who hurt the girls, she declared, before being led away.

That accusation was most convenient since Sarah Osborne was the next to be examined. She was a sickly woman and poor health had prevented her from attending church meeting in the Village for fourteen months. Despite her lapses from attending God's house, she would own nothing about a personal involve-ment with witchcraft. She denied having ever contracted with the devil to afflict the girls. She also disavowed any friendship with Sarah Good. She had not even seen the latter for two years. To the magistrates and spectators, however, her com-plicity in the black arts was all too apparent in the havoc she was wreaking in the meetinghouse at that very moment. While Os-borne stood before Hathorne and Corwin, the girls shrieked in agony as her specter darted among them, pinching, choking, and biting. Every girl affirmed that Osborne, dressed exactly as

(Plate 9; Site 22)
Tomb of the
Corwin Family,
Salem.

she now was before them, had tormented them also on previous occasions. Faced with such damning testimony, Osborne retreated somewhat and told of strange things that had happened to her; of being assaulted by "a thing like an indian all black which did pinch her in her neck," and of a voice that bid her not attend meeting. But to the charge of witchcraft she maintained her innocence. She told Hathorne "that shee was more like to be bewitched than that she was a witch." Frustrated, the magistrates ordered her removed and Tituba brought before them.

Since the episode of the witch cake, Tituba had seen rough treatment at the hands of her master, Reverend Parris. Increasingly convinced that witchcraft lay behind the girls' torments, Parris saw the root of that witchcraft in his Barbados slave. The only plausible explanation, after all, was the devil, and Parris beat Tituba until she told him, in private, what he wanted to hear: that she had been meddling with the powers of darkness. Now, before this Puritan throng, she had no reason to alter her story. The people gathered in the Salem Village meetinghouse on March 1 wanted a confession. Tituba was to give them one.

Tituba's confession was the critical event in the Salem tragedy. She alone knew of her secret sessions with the girls. Had she simply told the magistrates of those winter meetings at the parsonage, all suspicion of witchcraft would probably have ended there and the girls' antics punished instead of encouraged. She alone could stand up against the pack of maids who now lay tumbling about on the floor, naming her their present tormentor. Partly because she was confused and partly because of the whippings she had received from Parris, she confessed that she was a witch and implicated Good and Osborne as Satan's accomplices. From that day forth, Essex County was set on a collision course with disaster.

And so Tituba wove her tale. She told of a black dog that threatened her and ordered her to hurt the girls; of two large cats, one red, the other black, that bid her serve them, and of rides with Good and Osborne through the air on a pole. She said Good's familiar, a spectral creature that accompanied a witch on her diabolical missions, was a little yellow bird. Osborne had two creatures: a winged animal with the head of a woman and a second that was hairy and had a long nose. Tituba stated that Good and Osborne had forced her to attack the younger Ann Putnam with a knife the night before these very examinations. Ann corroborated the slave's account, saying that the witches had assaulted her and tried to cut off her head.

Had Tituba confined her accusations of witchhood to Good and Osborne, the repercussions of her testimony would have been less severe. But Tituba revealed much more. Most importantly, she told of a coven of witches in Massachusetts, six in number, led by a tall, white-haired man who dressed all in

(Plate 10; Site 2) Nathaniel Ingersoll's Ordinary, Danvers.

black. He was the leader of the witches in Essex County. Of the six witches, Tituba could name only two: Good and Osborne. The rest were unknown to her, she said, but they lived in the vicinity of Boston and Salem.

It appeared then that only a fraction of the malefactors causing the girls' torments had been brought to judgment. Their agonies would not cease until all the witches had been eradicated. The following day Hathorne and Corwin interrogated Tituba a second time, in hopes of discovering the name of the tall man. The woman simply took the opportunity to embellish her story. The tall man had come to her many times, she said, and had bid her sign her name in the devil's book. Finally, in the Village parsonage, she yielded and signed her name in blood. By Tituba's reckoning, nine persons were on the devil's roster. The list of Satan's servants was already growing.

From then until March 5, Tituba, Good, and Osborne were

reexamined. The last two still maintained their innocence, but who could ever believe them? The girls had spied the women's specters acting out their black deeds and Tituba, a confessed witch, had identified them as her companions. What greater proof was needed? Good, Osborne, and Tituba, however, were only minor characters in Satan's assault on New England. The magistrates knew that the forces of evil would not be halted until the tall man in black was apprehended. To aid them in their search they had only the help of the watchful eyes of the bewitched girls and the imagination of a slave.

On March 7 Tituba, Good, and Osborne were committed to the prison in Boston. Although the three malefactors were behind bars, the girls still complained of their specters traveling forth and tormenting them. To remedy this oversight, chains of iron were placed on Good and Osborne in order, it seems, to chain their specters as well. Osborne's constitution was too frail to undergo such harsh treatment. She died in prison on May 10, the first victim. Good, still unrepentant, would later come to

(Plate 11; Site 3) Site of the Salem Village Meetinghouse, Danvers.

trial. In the meantime she begged tobacco for her pipe from passersby who came to gawk at the accused witches.

Things were to be different with Tituba. As a confessing witch, she had a window into the invisible world shared only by the afflicted girls. The magistrates, for their part, had no reason to doubt the validity of her tale. She had told it often, and with each telling the details had remained unchanged. Moreover, her story dovetailed exactly with the girls' version, a matter which, in retrospect, should have come as no great surprise since they had been present at Tituba's earlier examinations. Lastly, Tituba herself soon became afflicted by the specters of the very witches she had exposed. As long as she could continue to identify Satan's followers in Massachusetts Bay, she would remain invaluable to the Puritan authorities.

The entire Salem episode had been acted out in miniature in the early days of March 1692. When others would be accused of the crime of witchcraft thereafter, they would have one of two choices: to maintain their innocence and thus follow Good and Osborne or, like Tituba, confess themselves witches. Were they to take the latter course, they would have to incriminate not only themselves but others. There was no need to spare the life of a confessing witch unless that person could further the course of justice in locating Satan's cohorts. To some in New England, however, this relying on the testimony of a confessing witch smacked of taking the devil's evidence as truth. For the moment their voices were silent.

Tituba's confession had one final, terrible effect. It had given unquestionable credibility to the accusations made by the afflicted girls. The one person who could have revealed all had capitulated, thereby giving credence to the girls' claims of the spectral sight which permitted them to identify witches. Both accusers and confessor had so intertwined their bizarre tales that, together with the physical agonies the girls endured, it became impossible not to believe them. Mere mortals, magistrates and citizens alike, could not witness the invisible events these girls perceived. Believing the girls' stories and their accusations would be the only way to rein in the forces of evil. It would be a high price to pay.

On Friday, March 11, Parris met with his fellow ministers at the parsonage in Salem Village for a solemn day of prayer concerning the recent infestation of witches. The girls were also present. They remained calm except when prayers concluded, at which point their moanings and contortions would resume. No doubt the ministers pressed them for the identity of the remaining witches. On the following day, these efforts were rewarded. Young Ann Putnam's eyes were opened and a fourth witch exposed. Her name was Martha Corey.

Martha Corey was no ordinary witch. Unlike the three who had been accused before her, she was a church member of Parris's own congregation and a tireless attendant at meeting. She was the third wife of Giles Corey (Site 16c; Plate 12), a landowner and a brute of a man. Martha had had the irreverence to oppose the entire witchcraft proceedings. She referred to the afflicted girls as "distracted persons," refusing to believe they were bewitched. She had even removed the saddle from her husband's horse to prevent his riding off to attend the examinations in the Village; but he went anyway.

It was one matter for the girls to cry out on three pariahs. It was another matter to accuse a person of Corey's standing. Accordingly, the authorities acted more discreetly. On the same day that the girls complained of Martha as their newest tormentor, Edward Putnam, Ann's uncle, and Ezekiel Cheever rode out to Salem Farms to inform Martha that she had been accused and to hear what she would say in answer. Before departing, the two men asked young Ann Putnam to tell them what clothes Martha's specter was wearing. They hoped that Martha herself would be differently attired, thus proving that Ann was mistaken in the person she saw. Alas, she could not answer them, Ann said, because the witch Corey had temporarily removed her spectral sight.

Putnam and Cheever found Martha alone in her house. When they entered, she looked up smiling and told them she knew why they had come. "You are come to talke with me about being a witch but I am none. I cannot helpe people's talking of me," she said. Putnam told her that they had come only to talk with her because she had that day been accused. Before they could say more, however, Martha taunted them saying, "Does shee tell you what cloathes I have on?" It appeared that Martha magically knew of their conversation with young Ann. How else would she have known the substance of that talk and the purpose behind this visit? Martha's own statements proved her a witch. Confronted with this, she made little reply but smiled "as if shee had showed us a pretty trick," the men later reported. Corey then upbraided them saying that the authorities should "stop the mouthes of people that they might not say thus of her."

In reality, the reverse occurred. The voices accusing Martha Corey of being a witch increased in number. On March 14, she visited the Thomas Putnam household at the latter's request to see Putnam's daughter Ann who had first cried out against her. When Martha entered the house, however, young Ann fell into grievous fits, her limbs writhing, her tongue protruding from her mouth and her eyes blinded. She accused Martha of feeding her familiar, a little yellow bird, between her index and middle fingers. Moments later Ann Putnam reported seeing Corey's specter roasting a spectral man over a spectral fire. Pandemonium broke loose. Mercy Lewis, who was also present in the room, fell into a fit as well and cried that other witches had arrived. These tempted her to write in the devil's book. The Putnams asked Martha to leave and she did so; but Satan's work was not yet finished. The men of the household spent the remainder of the evening restraining Lewis, so that unseen hands would not drag her into the fire.

If there had been doubts about Martha Corey before, these were swept away in the aftermath of the incident at Thomas Putnam's. By week's end the entire pack of girls was accusing her of having assailed them, and Abigail Williams deposed that she had seen Martha at the devil's sacrament. On Saturday, March 19, Hathorne and Corwin signed the warrant for Martha's arrest. Because the Sabbath was the following day and warrants could not be served on the Sabbath, Martha remained free one day longer.

That Sunday, as she had done on so many other Sundays be-

(Plate 12; Site 16c)
Grave of Mary Corey,
Salem.

fore, Martha attended the Village meeting. The church members were outraged. Here was an accused witch making a mockery of their service by her presence in God's house. Without a warrant, however, the good people of Salem Village could do nothing but permit Martha her usual seat. The afflicted girls, also in attendance, had no such restraints. When they realized that Corey was present they went into a frenzy. The visiting Reverend Deodat Lawson was scheduled to speak but because of the turmoil, he could hardly preach the sermon he had prepared. In the middle of the service, eleven-year-old Abigail Williams leapt to her feet and demanded of Lawson in a loud voice, "Now stand up, and Name your Text!" When Lawson answered her she sneered, "It is a long Text." Were there any devils in Salem Village, Abigail Williams was certainly among them. In the afternoon meeting she announced that Martha

(Plate 13; Site 27)
Grave of Constable
Joseph Herrick,
Beverly.

Corey's apparition was sitting on a beam of the meetinghouse, feeding her yellow bird between her fingers.

At noon on Monday, March 21, Constable Joseph Herrick (Site 27; Plate 13) brought Martha Corey to the Village meetinghouse to be examined at last. Martha had claimed that her testimony would open the eyes of the magistrates and expose the delusion which had befallen Essex County. She was wrong. No use of reason could explain away the torments the girls suffered when Martha stood before them that afternoon. The examination opened with the Reverend Nicholas Noyes of Salem Town delivering "a very pertinent and pathetic Prayer." Then Hathorne asked Martha why she hurt the maids. "I do not," she answered tersely.

Martha denied any dealings in the blacks arts, but the girls refuted her denials. They asserted that Martha's shape, invisible to all save the afflicted, had brought them the devil's book. On other occasions Martha's specter had choked, pinched, and strangled them. "I never had to do with Witchcraft," Martha protested, "I am a Gospel Woman," to which the girls replied that she was a Gospel witch. "We must not beleive all that these distracted children say," Corey protested, addressing herself to the magistrates. Hathorne and Noyes replied that "it was the judgment of all that were present, they [the girls] were Bewitched, and only she, the Accused Person said, they were Distracted."

Then the entire assembly witnessed a terrifying example of the devil's choreography. Whatever movement Martha made, the girls mimicked her. When Martha bit her lip the girls shrieked of being bitten on their arms and wrists and rushed to the magistrates to show them the teeth marks in their flesh. When Martha pinched her fingers or grasped one hand in another the girls screamed that Corey pinched and showed the authorities their bruises. Mrs. Gertrude Pope, a newcomer to the accusing circle, complained of Corey's causing terrible pains in her abdomen; it felt as if her bowels were being torn out. She took her muff and threw it at Martha. Missing, she removed a shoe and struck the woman a blow on the head. And when Martha stirred her feet, the girls stamped with their own so forcefully that the building quaked. "I beleive it is apparent she practiseth Witchcraft in the congregation," Noyes declared. No one save Martha Corey objected to his comment. "If you will all go hang me, how can I help it?" she asked. For the final time, Martha's ability to foretell the future would prove true. The Puritans of Salem Village intended just that. She was taken away to prison in Salem to await trial.

Even before Martha Corey's examination, the girls had begun to complain of a new witch who tormented them. She appeared first to young Ann Putnam on March 13, the day after Martha Corey was exposed. This latest witch pinched and choked poor Ann and urged her to sign the devil's book. Ann recognized the shape as a member of the Village church; but she did not know the specter's name. That information was short in coming. Later in the week, Ann's mother and Mercy Lewis revealed that the woman was Rebecca Nurse, a seventy-one-year-old matriarch of the church, respected in the community for her piety and years of Christian service.

It was a measure of how uncontrollable the situation in Salem Village had become that a woman of Rebecca Nurse's stature should even be considered a candidate for witchhood. Had the girls first accused Rebecca Nurse or Martha Corey of witchcraft instead of Tituba, Good, and Osborne, the authorities would probably have dismissed their ravings as deranged folly. For the moment, the tide of events and circumstances was flowing with the girls' outcries and against the safety and peace of the people of Essex County.

Rebecca lived with her husband, Francis, and their large family on a farm of three hundred acres (Site 6; Plate 14) located not far from the Village center. She had raised her children in a Christian home and in the process had impressed her neighbors with her gentleness and kindness. Now, in 1692, weak with infirmities and gradually growing deaf, she desired nothing more than to enjoy the tranquility of her twilight years.

It was not to be so. Although she had numerous friends, Rebecca also had enemies. Many years before, when a neighbor's swine had uprooted her garden, she had berated the owner in harsh terms. Mysteriously, the man had died a slow death shortly thereafter, with convulsions similar to those now experienced by the afflicted girls. His widow, Sarah Holten (Site 5; Plate 15), could not help but notice the similarity. And Rebecca had a more sinister enemy in Ann Putnam, Sr.

The elder Ann had finally achieved the position of vengeance she desired: membership in the ranks of the afflicted. On March 19, the specters of Rebecca Nurse and Martha Corey had assailed her, she afterward declared, "with such tortors as no toungu can Express because I would not yeald to their Hellish temtations" to sign the devil's book. Three nights later Rebecca's shape returned alone and urged her to sign, threatening to tear the soul out of her body if she refused, and blasphemously denying the grace of God and the truth of the scriptures.

(Plate 14; Site 6) Rebecca Nurse House, Danvers.

(Plate 15; Site 5) Sarah Holten House, Danvers.

The shape of Rebecca did not confine itself to molesting Ann Putnam, Sr. By March 23, most of the accusing girls had identified Rebecca as their torturer on previous occasions. Four days earlier, in the Parris household, Rebecca's specter had approached Abigail Williams and offered her the book. "I won't, I won't, I won't take it, I do not know what Book it is: I am sure it is none of God's Book, it is the Divels Book, for ought I know," Abigail had replied to the specter. Within half a week, Mary Walcott and Elizabeth Hubbard added their voices to those saying Rebecca was a witch. On the complaints of the accusing circle, Hathorne and Corwin issued a warrant for Nurse's arrest.

When the outcries against Rebecca had barely begun, Israel and Elizabeth Porter, friends of the Nurses, visited the Nurse farm to inform Rebecca that she had been named among the accused. The old woman was ill, had been bedridden for over a week, and was totally unaware that the girls were proclaiming her in league with the devil. She asked about the afflicted girls, saying that she had intended to visit them, but feared a recurrence of fits that she had suffered in her younger days. Rebecca worried, too, that some of the accused were innocent. When the Porters informed her that she was among the accused witches, Rebecca was dumbfounded. "The will of the Lord be done," she said resignedly. Then her Puritan resilience returned. "As to this thing I am Innocent as the child unborne but seurly . . . what sine [sin] hath god found out in me unrepented of that he should Lay such an Affliction upon me In my old Age?" she asked. The Porters had no answer to her question.

On the morning of Thursday, March 24, Rebecca was brought before Hathorne and Corwin to answer the girls' accusations. The girls were present as usual, and the examination began with them already in convulsions. Ann Putnam, Jr. cried that Rebecca's shape hurt her; another said that she had been beaten by Nurse's specter that very morning. "What do you say to it?" Hathorne demanded of her. "I can say before my Eternal father I am innocent, & God will clear my innocency," came her unwavering reply. The elder Ann Putnam testified that Rebecca had brought her the devil's book and, turning to the old woman, shrieked, "Did you not bring the Black man with you? Did you not bid me tempt God & dye? How oft have you eat and drunk y'r own damnation?" Overcome by the bedlam, Rebecca moaned, "Oh, Lord, help me," in answer to the charge.

Badger and accuse her as they did, Rebecca nonetheless held fast to her convictions. When Hathorne asked her if she had familiarity with any spirits she answered, "None but with God alone." The magistrates wondered how she could stand there charged with witchcraft and yet shed no tears of remorse or pity for the afflicted. "You do not know my heart," she replied. But her denials were of no avail. The examination concluded as it had with Martha Corey before her, with the girls mimicking the woman's motions. When Rebecca moved her hands the girls were seized with violent fits; and when she tilted her head to one side the girls' heads were likewise tilted. Elizabeth Hubbard's head was twisted so oddly that Abigail Williams cried out, "Set up Goody Nurse's head. The maid's neck will be broke!" And when Rebecca's head was forced upright, Hubbard's head magically followed.

The magistrates committed Rebecca to Salem prison at day's end. But she was not the only accused witch jailed that day. The apparition of Dorcas Good, five-year-old daughter of Sarah, had been flying about the countryside since early March, pinching, choking, and offering the book to Mary Walcott and young Ann Putnam. Accordingly, this youngest of the witches in the Salem hysteria was examined by the magistrates. The small child admitted that she was a witch and that her mother had made her one. She, too, was incarcerated.

The examinations of Corey and Nurse confirmed public opinion that the afflicted girls were God's chosen instruments in the battle with the forces of darkness. The girls had demonstrated conclusively that witchcraft abounded. "Look to her! she will have a Fit presently," they had said about one of their group on many occasions; and behold it had come to pass. The fits were so violent and unnatural that those who witnessed them were convinced that the devil was at work. Reverend Lawson wrote that during the examination of Rebecca Nurse the torments of the afflicted were so hideous that "the whole assembly was struck with consternation, and they were afraid, that those that sate next to them, were under the influence of Witchcraft." The girls had also proven to be competent healers of the bewitched. They had been able to terminate fits simply by touching the afflicted person. In subsequent examinations this practice would evolve into the famed "touch test," whereby an accused person's ability to bring an afflicted one out of her fits merely by touch was accepted evidence of witchcraft. Few realized how easily these acts could be feigned, in which case all innocent persons lay in the shadow of accusation.

That shadow now fell over the household of John Proctor of Salem Village (Site 13; Plate 16). Proctor had been an outspoken opponent of the proceedings from the beginning. Mary Warren, one of the afflicted girls, was maidservant in his house. Proctor had cured her fits by sitting her down at a spinning wheel and promising to thrash her if she stirred. When John Indian, Tituba's husband, became one of the tormented circle in

(Plate 16; Site 13) John Proctor House, Peabody.

early April, Proctor angrily remarked to a neighbor "that if mr Parish [Parris] would let him have his Indian hee . . . would soone Drive the Divell out of him." And the day after Rebecca Nurse was examined, Proctor declared that if the girls "were let alone so we should all be Devils & witches quickly." His criticism did not escape the girls' sensitive ears. In late March they turned their spectral sight and vengeance upon him and his family.

On March 28, at Ingersoll's ordinary in Salem Village, one of the afflicted girls announced that she spied the specter of Elizabeth Proctor, John's wife, hovering about the room. "Old witch," said the girl, "I'll have her hang." A witness to the accusation, twenty-six-year-old William Rayment, told the girl that he believed she lied for he saw nothing at all. Whereupon the girl, somewhat ashamedly, retracted her statement saying "that she did it for sport."

By early April, the girls' hunger for accusation had become insatiable. They declared that they had seen the devil's sacrament at a house in the Village where those gathered partook of red bread and red drink. Already two church members had been exposed as witches and Elizabeth Proctor, who stood in high regard in the community, was being denounced by an ever-increasing number of the girls. Faced with these terrible facts, Reverend Parris girded himself and prepared a sermon which would serve warning to those in Massachusetts who would meddle with Satan.

In the Village meeting on Sunday, April 3, Parris began his lecture with a verse from the Book of John: "Have I not chosen you twelve and one of you is a devil?" He got no further. Immediately after he finished the verse, Sarah Cloyce, wife of Peter Cloyce of Salem Village and sister to Rebecca Nurse, stormed out of the assembly, the door slamming loudly behind her. It was an exit guaranteed to arouse suspicion. So it came as little surprise when, later in the day, the girls again fell into fits and saw Sarah's specter with a host of other witches present at the devil's sacrament. "Oh Goodwife Cloyce," the girls moaned to the shape, "I did not think to see you here! . . . Is this a time to receive the Sacrament, you ran-away on the Lords-Day, and scorned to receive it in the Meeting-House, and, Is this a time to receive it? I wonder at you!"

On April 8, a warrant was issued for the arrest of Elizabeth Proctor and Sarah Cloyce for practicing witchcraft upon the bodies of Abigail Williams, John Indian, Mary Walcott, Ann Putnam, Jr., and Mercy Lewis, who collectively "Craved Justice" from the authorities. The two women were examined on April 11, but on this occasion the examinations were held in the meetinghouse in Salem Town (Site 15; Plate 17) to accommodate several leading figures of the colony, including Deputy Governor Thomas Danforth and Captain Samuel Sewall (Site 39; Plate 18), who had ridden out from Boston to obtain a closer view of the witchcraft proceedings. John Proctor accompanied his wife to her interrogation by the magistrates to comfort and defend her. With the examinations now removed from backward Salem Village, perhaps reason would at last prevail. The best minds in Massachusetts would be present: men who surely would not believe the ridiculous fabrications which Hathorne and Corwin had accepted in committing persons to prison.

As it turned out, although the site had changed, the basic framework of the examination had not. The authorities asked the same guilt-presuming questions they had before. The afflicted still peered into space and saw the specters that beset their company with terrible agonies. Danforth first directed his inquiries to John Indian who had complained of Proctor's and Cloyce's assaults on him. "Who hurt you?" he demanded of the slave. "Goody Procter first, and then Goody Cloyse," came the reply. But Sarah would have none of his story. "You are a grievous liar!" she yelled at her accuser. Still, the evidence weighed heavily against her. Mary Walcott testified that Sarah had brought her the book. Abigail Williams stated that Sarah had been present at a devil's sacrament with over forty other witches, so numerous had Satan's followers become. There Sarah's apparition had had the courtesy to incriminate itself, telling Abigail that the witches drank their victims' blood twice a day. Sarah, exhausted from the questioning and near fainting,

(Plate 17; Site 15)
Site of the
Meetinghouse of the
First Church in Salem,
Salem.

collapsed in a chair. The girls said that her spirit had left her
body to visit her sister Rebecca in prison.

The focus of the examination now shifted to Elizabeth Proctor. "Does she hurt you?" Danforth asked the girls. For the moment they could not answer, struck dumb by the witch Proctor.
Not even Abigail Williams could spew her lies; her hand had
been thrust into her own mouth. Finally, John Indian broke the
silence. "This is the woman that came in her shift and choked
me," he bellowed. "I take God in heaven to be my witness, that
I know nothing of it," came Elizabeth's cool response. When
she merely looked at the afflicted persons they fell into convulsions. Then Abigail recovered her tongue. Elizabeth had come
to her with the book, she said. "Did not you . . . tell me, that
your maid had written [i.e., signed the book]?" she asked the

(Plate 18; Site 39) Tomb of Captain Samuel Sewall, Boston.

woman. "Dear Child, it is not so. There is another judgement, dear child," Elizabeth replied.

By now the whirlwind of accusation had engulfed John Proctor. Abigail Williams and young Ann Putnam caught sight of his shape sitting on a beam of the meetinghouse. Abigail shouted that Proctor's shape was moving toward Mrs. Pope, the same woman who had struck Martha Corey with her shoe, and immediately thereafter Mrs. Pope fell into a fit. Proctor proclaimed his innocence; but he should have saved his voice. His apparition was everywhere: tormenting the girls, sitting calmly in the magistrates' laps and straddling the back of a dog which had strayed into the room. What choice did the authorities have other than commit the three to prison, Sarah Cloyce and the Proctors, husband and wife?

There had been something malicious in Abigail Williams's charge that Elizabeth Proctor had forced her maid to sign the devil's book. For the Proctors' maid was none other than the afflicted Mary Warren. Abigail's outburst against her on April 11 indicated that after a month and a half of witch hunting, a rift had developed within the circle of accusing girls.

Mary's defection from the group occurred in April, around the time when the girls turned their spectral sight upon her master and mistress. Although Mary felt little regard for Elizabeth, she had a great deal of respect and affection for John Proctor. It was one matter for the girls to destroy other people with their lies; but when the Proctors were likewise accused, Mary caught a fleeting glimpse of reality. The girls did "dissemble" in their fits, she told the magistrates. To others she likened their ravings to the mumblings of "Keyser's daughter," a local woman who had been mentally deranged for many years.

If Mary thought that her desertion would discredit the testimony of the afflicted girls, she was mistaken. When they discovered that her statements were undermining their credibility before the magistrates, the girls adopted a simple and unassailable solution: they accused Mary of having signed the devil's book, thus identifying her as one of their tormentors. Before long, the entire group was crying that Mary's apparition had appeared to them offering the book and choking those who refused to sign. The scheme worked. Although the magistrates and witnesses could not see Mary's shape as it tormented the remaining girls, the agonies which the latter endured was sufficient proof that she had joined the forces of darkness. Witches had brought her the book on so many occasions, the magistrates reasoned, that it did not seem improbable that the girl had succumbed to temptation and signed. A warrant was issued for her arrest, and on April 19 she was carted off to Salem Village to appear before Hathorne and Corwin, now one accused of witchcraft rather than an accuser.

But Mary Warren was not alone at Ingersoll's ordinary on the morning of the nineteenth. The afflicted persons had spent the intervening days peering into their world of shapes, straining their eyes to identify new witches. Caught up in the hysteria of the community and basking in the awe and attention of all of Essex County, the girls now exposed witches on a routine basis.

And with each accusation and arrest, their appetite for notoriety increased. Few people in all Massachusetts Bay could refute the girls' slanders. With their venomous charges they could destroy in an instant the respect normally held for a good and honest person. No man, neither the country farmer nor the learned theologian, could stand against them. What credible defense was possible against evidence which could not be seen? As long as the authorities believed the tales of specters, no innocent person was immune to the cry of accusation. Men like John Proctor, who had opposed the girls' testimony, suffered the accusers' wrath.

The three persons brought to Salem Village with Mary Warren were Giles Corey, Bridget Bishop, and Abigail Hobbs. Eighty-year-old Giles Corey, husband of the imprisoned Martha, was a powerful man and feared by many in the Village. Seventeen years before he had brutally murdered a servant on his farm and ever since had tangled repeatedly with the law. Bridget Bishop had long been accounted a witch. Around 1678 a neighbor had charged her with witchcraft, and although he later retracted his accusation, the memory of the event persisted. Now in 1692, when the girls repeated the charge, there were many who would attest to its truthfulness and give witness against her. She had done little to endear herself to her neighbors: in this Puritan community she had had the effrontery to entertain people in her house (Site 12; Plate 19) at all hours of the night, drinking and playing shuffleboard. Many worried that her behavior would corrupt the youth of the area. And she dressed in a flashy "red paragon bodice" decorated with lace. Rumor and suspicion had always followed her. The cry of witch was never far behind.

Abigail Hobbs was the mentally unbalanced daughter of William and Deliverance Hobbs of Topsfield. It was said that she often slept alone at night in the woods near her house, something no sane Puritan woman would have attempted. Moreover, she was downright rude. Once, while visiting friends with her mother, she announced that her mother was not baptized. Then, to correct this oversight, she sprinkled Deliverance with water, babbling all the while that she baptized her "in the name of the father son and Holy Ghost." Now, on April 19, her worthless thoughts would pour forth. Her revelations would make Tituba's pale by comparison.

Abigail was probably the first to be examined that morning. She glibly confessed herself a witch. This should have come as no surprise from a woman who, a year before, had been mad enough to remark of her own free will that "She had Sold her selfe boddy & Soull to the old boy." She told Hathorne of seeing "things like men" which came to her with a book, asking her to sign. She did so in exchange for fine clothes which the men promised to deliver. As matters turned out, they reneged; she never received the clothing. She also confessed her bargain with the devil that he could appear to the girls in her shape to afflict them. Her words were a vindication for the magistrates. They had thus far been pursuing witches solely with the girls' spectral vision. Here at last was one who explained the devil's mysteries and how the shapes came to be. Unfortunately, she went be-

(Plate 19; Site 12) Bridget Bishop House, Danvers.

yond personal incrimination and named several of her witch confederates which gave new impetus to the accusations.

When Giles Corey was examined, he denied any involvement in witchcraft. He had given testimony against his wife in March, believing the cries of the afflicted instead of Martha's defense. When the girls accused him, his resolution returned. He knew he was innocent. But he could not explain the bizarre events which took place around him. When his hands were free, the girls fell into fits and complained of being pinched. "What!" Hathorne demanded of the man, "Is it not enough to act witchcraft at other times, but must you do it now, in face of authority?" "I am a poor creature, and cannot help it," came Corey's confused reply. They commanded the marshal to bind his hands. Despite this precaution, his specter still worked its evil magic. When he tilted his head to one side, the afflicteds' heads were likewise tilted; when he sucked in his cheeks, theirs were sucked in as well. It was obvious to all present that Corey was a wizard.

Mary Warren was brought in next. She was no longer one of the annointed accusers. Barely a month before she had sat where they now sat and screamed mightily with the rest that Rebecca Nurse's shape went among them. Now she faced the other side of justice. She proclaimed her innocence to the assembly; but with the other girls, John Indian, and Mrs. Pope tumbling about her, her determination dissolved. Her fits returned. She fell to the floor, convulsing. Some of the girls cried that Mary had been about to confess to having signed the book when the shapes of Martha Corey and John and Elizabeth Proctor appeared and struck her down, saying that she should reveal nothing. Examining her that morning proved a fruitless venture. Whenever she would start into her explanation, she was seized with a terrible fit which prevented interrogation. All was not in vain, however. The Reverend Samuel Parris, who was present that day, noted that when Mary started confessing, the afflicted girls came out of their fits. Here was valuable proof that Mary had enlisted with the devil as the girls had claimed.

Since Mary Warren's fits prevented her examination, she was

removed from the chamber and replaced by Bridget Bishop. When Bridget entered the room, all the girls fell into fits. They accused her pointblank of hurting them. Mary Walcott shouted that she spied Bridget's specter and pointed to the spot where it stood. Although no one else could see the invisible shape, Mary's brother, Jonathan Walcott, took hold of his sword and struck the place where she pointed. Mary saw the sword rip the specter's cloak and heard the cloth tear. Before the entire assembly Bridget's garments were searched and a tear found "that seems to answere what was alledged." "I am innocent to a Witch," Bridget told the magistrates. "I know not what a Witch is." If she did not know what a witch was, Hathorne asked her, then how could she be certain she was not? "If I were any such person you should know it," Bridget shot back menacingly. "I am not come here to say I am a witch to take away my life." But there was no need for a confession. That she was a witch had already been established by the torments the girls endured in Bridget's presence. She and the three who had been examined before her were committed to prison in Salem Town.

The following day, the magistrates visited Mary Warren and Abigail Hobbs in jail to examine them a second time. Mary had regained the use of her tongue and proceeded to use it, adding her voice to those declaring her mistress Elizabeth a witch. She also confirmed the girls' accusations that Giles Corey was a wizard. When Corey, who was imprisoned with her, was brought to her cell so that she might accuse him directly, Mary fell "into a dreadful fit again, and upon her Recovery Charged him to his face with being the procurer of it." She who had once declared that the afflicted girls "did but dissemble" in their torments had now come full circle. The only way she could remove herself from suspicion of witchcraft was to rejoin the accusers. And to accomplish that she had to confirm everything they said.

Abigail Hobbs regaled the magistrates with even more wonders of the invisible world. The apparition of Sarah Good had appeared to her two days before, she said, urging her to flee. The witches feared that Abigail would confess all and destroy Satan's great plan to subvert the Church in Massachusetts.

Abigail had refused the request. On another occasion, the devil had come to her in the shape of a man carrying wooden dolls bearing the likenesses of Abigail Williams and young Ann Putnam. He ordered her to prick the dolls with a thorn. When she did as he commanded, he told her that the girls in question were simultaneously tormented. She claimed that she had been one of many present at the devil's sacrament, feasting on red bread and red wine. Her tale, coupled with the renewed energies of the afflicted girls, prompted a rash of fresh accusations.

On April 21, nine persons were arrested and charged with witchcraft: an ancient man named Nehemiah Abbot; William and Deliverance Hobbs, Abigail's parents; Edward Bishop, stepson of Bridget Bishop, and his wife, Sarah, both of Salem Village; Mary Easty, wife of Isaac Easty and sister to Rebecca Nurse and Sarah Cloyce; Mary Black, a negro slave in the household of Nathaniel Putnam; Sarah Wilds, wife of John Wilds; and Mary English, wife of the wealthy Salem merchant, Philip English. Of these, five were residents of Topsfield: Easty, Wilds, Abbot, and the Hobbses. Until now the accusations had been confined largely to persons living in the vicinity of Salem Village. Abigail Hobbs had changed that. Her gossip and stories had furnished the afflicted girls with a host of new suspects. They wasted no time in crying out against the likeliest Topsfield candidates for witchhood. The contagion had begun to spread.

The nine accused were taken to Salem Village on April 22 and led before the magistrates to face what by now had become a familiar scene. When the prisoner entered the room, the afflicted girls fell into fits, crying that the accused tormented them. Then the prisoner was placed about eight feet from a bar of justice, behind which were seated the magistrates. The girls occupied a position between the magistrates and the accused. Constables stood by the prisoner, holding her hands lest she employ them to pinch the children. An additional safeguard had recently been added. Throughout the entire examination the accused was directed to look only upon the magistrates; for whenever her eyes wandered to the girls, they immediately complained of being tormented. Indeed, it was now accepted as partial proof of witchcraft if a mere glance from the accused sent the girls into convulsions. And at the conclusion of the examination each prisoner was put through a final acid test: reciting the Lord's Prayer. It was commonly believed that the devil could not recite the prayer without making an unforgivable error in content or pronunciation which transformed the act from holiness to blasphemy. Even the slightest mistake, such as pronouncing "hollowed" instead of "hallowed," was evidence that the accused was a witch.

Nehemiah Abbot had the singular distinction of being the only person the girls accused whom they also acquitted. At his examination, Mary Walcott and young Ann Putnam swore that his specter had assailed them. Ann even spied Abbot's apparition perched on the now-familiar beam, which evidently served as a convenient resting place for these witch shapes. Then the girls' conviction deserted them. They wavered in their accusation. The shape which had afflicted them was similar to Abbot's in appearance, they said, but they could not be sure. "Charge him not unless it be he," Hathorne instructed them. The girls gathered around the old man, talking with him and examining his features. They concluded that they had been mistaken; it was not the man. If their retraction had been a conscious one, then it was a clever ploy. People had begun to wonder why the girls' spectral sight had thus far acquitted no one. But here the girls demonstrated that they could discern a witch from an innocent person; they would not allow a guiltless person to be accused of witchcraft. Or so the populace now thought. The old man was dismissed.

The others were not so fortunate. Edward Bishop and wife were guilty by association since Edward's stepmother had already been accused. When the Parrises' servant, John Indian, had lain convulsing at a previous examination, Edward had cured the slave's fits by striking him with a cane, prescribing the same treatment for the afflicted girls as well. Like Proctor before him, he had opposed the girls; like Proctor he now felt their wrath. He and his wife were examined and committed to prison.

Deliverance and William Hobbs stood accused by their own

daughter. Deliverance, in particular, was awestruck by the tumult about her. She initially denied any involvement in witchcraft, but the magistrates bullied and cajoled her into confessing. They were aided by Abigail Williams. The little girl announced loudly that although she could see Deliverance's specter upon the beam, she could not see the poor defendant standing before the magistrates. But her glance was potent: whichever girl she looked upon fell into fits. "Have you signed to any book?" Hathorne demanded of her. "It is very lately then. The night before the last," came her broken reply. To make her confession credible she spoke more lies. The shape of Sarah Wilds had brought the book to her, she said. Wilds had also appeared with Sarah Osborne, carrying dolls with pins to prick them, and commanding Deliverance to do so. As Deliverance concocted her confession, a familiar eerie stillness passed over the assembly. Whenever a witch confessed, the afflicted girls experienced temporary relief.

Her husband, William, was more recalcitrant: he could not be goaded into confession. "I am clear of any Witch," he told the magistrates. But evidence to the contrary occurred before his very eyes. His glance leveled the girls, knocking them all to the floor. Abigail Williams saw his shape passing from girl to girl, torturing each. When it became known that William had not attended church meeting for a "pretty while," Hathorne rebuked him, "If you put away God's ordinances, no wonder that the Devil prevails with you." William remained obstinate. He would not even admit that the afflicted persons seemed bewitched. It must have been exceedingly bitter then to have been committed to prison with his wife and daughter who had steadfastly maintained the contrary.

Mary Black was an unwitting creature who failed to comprehend what was asked of her. Had she been a different sort, she could have wreaked as much destruction upon the community as had Tituba. She denied hurting anyone. When asked if she pricked dolls with pins she answered that she pinned only her neckcloth. The magistrates ordered a demonstration, and when she gave one, several of the girls screamed with pain. Mary

Walcott had been so badly pricked in the arm by Black's specter that she bled. It was a diabolical demonstration convincing enough to have Mary imprisoned as well.

Sarah Wilds had little chance of clearing herself after Deliverance and Abigail Hobbs had named her a witch. Moreover, rumors of witchcraft had followed her for some time. Fifteen years before, a neighbor in Topsfield had accused Sarah of torturing and bewitching her. In the face of such damning testimony, she struggled to acquit herself. The girls saw her shape on the beam and screamed of being tormented by her. "I am not guilty, Sir," was all Sarah could say to the charges. It was not enough. So long as this hysteria reigned in Massachusetts denials would go unheeded.

Of those examined on April 22, Mary Easty of Topsfield was the most significant. Her sisters, Rebecca Nurse and Sarah Cloyce, were already in prison on the charge of witchcraft. Some people whispered that all three were witches and had been made so by their mother. Under such circumstances it was inevitable that Mary also be accused. Like her sisters, she protested her innocence. "I am clear of this sin," she told Hathorne who had pressed her to confess. The girls' antics spoke otherwise. Mary Walcott and Ann Putnam declared that they had seen Mary's shape in company with the newly confessed Deliverance Hobbs. But Mary was so adamant in her denials that even Hathorne hesitated. "Are you certain this is the woman?" he asked the girls. They were unable to answer him; a devil had prevented their talking. Finally, Ann Putnam, Jr. and Elizabeth Hubbard burst out, "Oh. Goody Easty, Goody Easty you are the woman, you are the woman!" Hathorne, incensed at Easty's intransigence, asked her if she thought the girls bewitched. "It is an evil spirit," she replied, "but wither it be witchcraft I do not know." No truer answer could have been spoken. Whatever evil spirit was at work in the girls, it could only bring ruin to Essex County.

Mary was imprisoned like the rest. But she would be allowed a brief respite. In the ensuing weeks, the girls began to doubt that they had ever seen Mary's specter; perhaps they had been mistaken. When the magistrates learned of this they questioned the girls. Only Mercy Lewis now said that she saw Mary's shape; the others were strangely silent or denied seeing Mary's apparition. This was not sufficient evidence to keep her imprisoned. And so, on May 18, she was released.

Her freedom was short-lived. When Mary was freed, Mercy Lewis fell into terrible convulsions. So horrible were her agonies that onlookers believed "shee could not continue long in this world." They sent for those infamous witch hunters, Abigail Williams, Ann Putnam, Jr., and Elizabeth Hubbard. The three girls hurried over, and training their spectral sight upon Mercy's contorted body, they spied Mary Easty's shape choking the poor girl. Hours later, Mercy regained consciousness. She told those gathered that Easty had tried to murder her because she alone had steadfastly maintained that Easty was a witch; the specter had returned to eliminate this last witness against her. New warrants were issued for Mary's arrest on May 20. She was examined at the house of Thomas Beadle in Salem and afterwards imprisoned. It would not be the last time that Mary's shape would roam the land, however. She would appear once more, months later, in a final revelation which would help bring the madness to a close.

Now, in late April, those times seemed far away. The list of accused persons increased with every passing day. The girls, those official bloodhounds in the apprehension of witches, knew their mission: the exposing of Satan's servants. As long as they could deliver names, they served a useful purpose to the authorities. To remain in the focus of attention, they had to discover new witches which they did with pitiless fervor.

But accusers as well as accused were increasing in number. People outside the original circle of girls began complaining of witches afflicting them; they, too, acquired spectral sight. Neighbor rose up against neighbor. Whenever the girls accused a new person of witchcraft, there were always those willing to give testimony to strange coincidences they had noted about the accused, many in the distant past. One man who testified against Bridget Bishop stated that she once paid him money for work he had done for her; shortly after leaving her presence, he was astonished to find the money missing from his pocket. Obviously the witch Bishop had paid him in spectral coin. These coincidences seem trite, but in 1692 they were sufficient evidence of witchcraft.

The final addition to the accusing circle were those who themselves had been accused and had confessed. In retrospect, it is a measure of the Puritan constitution that throughout the entire hysteria, only fifty people confessed to the crime. This is remarkable considering the horrors they saw before them: a roomful of girls screaming in agony, rolling about on the ground, accusing them of witchcraft. Even more difficult to endure was the disbelief of loved ones. Often when a woman was accused, her spouse and children believed her a witch. They reasoned that the magistrates would not permit innocents to be accused and imprisoned. They would urge her to confess and cleanse her soul. Later, when it became apparent that those who confessed were not to be executed, relatives would encourage her to confess to save her very life. The value of a confessing witch existed only in her ability to accuse others. Confessors searched their minds for persons to denounce and, barring that, bolstered the girls' statements by confirming their accusations. Reverend John Hale, in his account of the witchcraft, later wrote that "that which chiefly carried on this matter [the witch hunt] to such an height, was the increasing of confessors till they amounted to near about Fifty." As such, they were accomplices in the tragedy which was to follow.

On Saturday, April 30, warrants for the arrests of six new witches were issued by Hathorne and Corwin. Four of these, Sarah Morey of Beverly, Lydia Dustin of Reading, Susannah Martin of Amesbury, and Dorcas Hoar of Beverly, were brought before the magistrates and the girls at Salem Village on the morning of May 2. Like those before them they faced the same antics performed by the girls and the same insinuating questions posed by the magistrates. The records of Morey's and Dustin's examinations have not survived to the present day. Sarah Morey was imprisoned from May 1692 to January 1693 when she was acquitted by the Superior Court. Lydia Dustin likewise languished in prison where she died on 10 March 1693, probably the last victim of the hysteria.

Dorcas Hoar had long been accounted a witch. Several years before she had confessed to Reverend Hale that she practiced fortune-telling. A neighbor, Mary Gage, had even seen Hoar's prophecies fulfilled. Dorcas had come to Mary and informed her that her child, then in good health, would not live long. Within a month the child became suddenly ill and died. Although Dorcas had since renounced her meddlings with prophecy, her neighbors remembered. In Puritan morality, fortune-telling was only slightly less grievous than outright witchcraft. Now she stood before the law, but despite the girls' wailing and screaming, Dorcas would not be budged. "I never hurt any child in my life," she stubbornly told the magistrates. When the girls shouted that the specter of a black man whispered advice in her ear, she turned on them. "Oh! you are liars, & God will stop the mouth of liars," she yelled.

Susannah Martin (Site 36; Plate 20) was even more defiant. Like Dorcas Hoar, many people had long suspected her of witchcraft. That mattered little to Susannah. "Let them think what they will," she told Hathorne, after he stressed to her that all those assembled to see her examination thought her a witch. She even did the unthinkable. With the girls tumbling about crying in pain, she had the impudence to laugh. Had more people laughed at the girls the events at Salem might have taken a different turn. The magistrates saw nothing funny in the girls' torments. "What do you laugh at it?" they demanded of the woman. "Well I may at such folly," she answered smartly. She declared that she did not think the girls were bewitched. Instead, she intimated that the girls might be lying. Her statements bordered on blasphemy. Yet she was strikingly close to the truth. "Pray God discover you, if you be guilty," Hathorne admonished her toward the close of her examination. In response Susannah said, "Amen. A false tongue will never make a guilty person," a reply which could serve as an epitaph to the entire Salem affair.

(Plate 20; Site 36)
Site of Susannah
Martin's House,
Amesbury.

The constables had been unable to locate Philip English who had also been accused with the four women. One of the wealthiest of Salem's citizens and a merchant by trade, English (Site 18) had gone into hiding in Boston when he heard that the girls cried out against him. His whereabouts did not remain secret for long. By the end of May, the authorities had tracked him down and had him arrested. He was examined on May 31 and thereafter imprisoned. He did not stay there long. When it became apparent to him that the girls' spectral evidence condemned innocent people, he escaped with his wife who had also been accused. Though he could save his life, he could not save his property. The statutes of England provided that a witch's possessions were forfeit to the Crown. Of his estate, valued at fifteen hundred pounds, English would recover only three hundred pounds once the hysteria was over.

The last of the six accused was the most memorable. He was the Reverend George Burroughs, a Harvard graduate and a former minister in Salem Village. His tenure there had not been pleasant. He had lost two of his wives (Site 9b) and had also acquired the enmity of the Putnams. In 1683 he was forced to leave. In 1692, Burroughs was living in Wells, Maine, then part of Massachusetts. Although nine years had elapsed, some of his former parishioners, particularly the elder Ann Putnam, had not forgotten him. The cry of witchcraft would be her vehicle for vengeance, and she would not hesitate to use it.

Actually, the younger Ann was the first to sight the minister's apparition. On the evening of April 20, while Burroughs's body was very much in Wells, his shape allegedly journeyed to Salem Village to rally the forces of evil. It could no longer roam about undetected, however; the girls' spectral eyes had been opened. Young Ann spied his shape and announced its presence to those gathered around her. "Oh dreadfull, dreadfull here is a minister com: what are Ministers wicthes [witches] to?" she asked the specter. Then she fell into a fit, screaming that the shape tortured her, bidding her to write in the book. She refused, begging the apparition to reveal its name. The shape told her its name was Burroughs and listed its numerous crimes: the murders of his two wives and Reverend Deodat Lawson's wife; the conversion of many people to witchcraft; and the murders of several soldiers of the colony's militia. Burroughs's specter was fond of boasting. It told young Ann "that he was above wicth for he was a conjurer." Here then was the ringleader of all the witches in Essex County. He had been exposed at last.

Although Burroughs was arrested on May 4, he was not examined until the ninth. Since he was a minister of the Lord, his examination was to be more discreet. It would be ill-advised to proclaim to all of Massachusetts that a minister was the mastermind behind Satan's plot to overthrow the Church. He was taken to Nathaniel Ingersoll's ordinary and questioned privately by John Hathorne, Jonathan Corwin, Samuel Sewall, and William Stoughton (Site 41; Plate 21), four of the most respected men in the province. All four men would sit on the court which would later condemn Burroughs to death by hanging.

Stoughton had ridden over to Salem from his native Dorchester to participate in Burroughs's examination. A bachelor at sixty-one, Stoughton had lived a life in the public service. Graduating from Harvard College in 1650, he had gone to England, returning after the restoration of Charles II. He had refused a church calling and concentrated his energies instead on governmental matters. He was a man of iron, unmoveable in his convictions. Burroughs, or any of the other accused, could expect little mercy from him. His epitaph describes him fittingly as "A most strenuous Opponent of Impiety and Vice." In 1692 the vice was witchcraft, and William Stoughton would take it upon himself personally to destroy this abomination in Massachusetts.

Now Burroughs, the man accused of being the witches' leader, stood before authority. Stoughton and the other magistrates questioned him closely concerning his faith. Burroughs could not remember the last time he had partaken of the sacrament although he told them he had recently been to church meetings in Boston and Charlestown. He owned that only the first of his seven children had been baptized, a damaging confession considering that Puritan theology dictated that any infant who died unbaptized was damned. Burroughs had dangerously neglected his religion, prime evidence for his having fallen into the devil's snare.

(Plate 21; Site 41) Tomb of Chief Justice William Stoughton, Dorchester.

After his private interview with the four magistrates, he was led before the pack of girls. They promptly fell into convulsions, crying that he tormented them and brought them the devil's book. When Burroughs looked upon the girls they fell to the floor. Grown men came forward with evidence about his extraordinary physical prowess. Burroughs, though small in stature, had always been exceedingly strong. At Harvard he had been one of the school's best athletes. But these men exaggerated his strength out of the world of reality and into the supernatural. William Wormwood testified that Burroughs had lifted a seven-foot musket by grasping it behind the firelock and raising his arm. Another swore that Burroughs told him he could lift a heavy barrel of molasses with one hand. Other witnesses appeared against him. They informed the magistrates that Burroughs had mistreated his first two wives and had forced one of them to sign a pact not to divulge his secrets. His great secret, his witchcraft, had at last come to light. He protested his innocence, but to those assembled it was evident that he was a wizard. He was imprisoned with the rest.

Although the ringleader had finally been caught, many of his followers were still at large. On May 10, warrants were issued for the arrest of three more witches. One of these, John Willard of Salem Village, fled to Lancaster where he was apprehended on the seventeenth. It was reported that when he was arrested the girls had a moment's relief from their torments. Willard had earlier aided in the arrests of several persons charged with witchcraft, but when he saw upstanding people accused, he refused to serve any more warrants. Shortly thereafter, the girls cried out against him. On May 18 he saw the antics that had damned those he had arrested turned against himself. The girls fell in a heap when he looked at them. Others said that the black man whispered in his ear, urging him not to confess. When the magistrates asked him to recite the Lord's Prayer, he was unable to do so, even after several attempts. "Well," he explained to the magistrates, "it is these wicked ones that do so overcome me." The magistrates had a different explanation. "It is no strange thing that God will not suffer a wizard to pray to him," they told the man accusingly. Willard, however, would not be cowed into confession. "If it was the last time I was to speak, I am innocent," he told them. He would maintain his innocence to the end.

Two other accused witches were arrested and examined on May 10 at Beadle's Tavern. They were George Jacobs, Sr. of Salem and his granddaughter Margaret. Old Jacobs was an early opponent of the witchcraft proceedings. He had had the opportunity to study the girls' afflictions firsthand, for the bewitched Sarah Churchill was maidservant in his household. He did not like what he had seen: the girls were "bitch witches," he said. The examination opened with Abigail Williams clearly identifying the old man as a wizard. Jacobs laughed in reply. But when he realized that the magistrates were in earnest he roared, "You tax me for a wizard, you may as well tax me for a buzard I have done no harm." The justices put him to the test of saying the Lord's Prayer and, fatally, he failed. Sarah Churchill, saying that she had seen his name in the devil's book, urged him to confess. He denied it: "Well burn me, or hang me, I will stand in the truth of Christ, I know nothing of it."

Sarah Churchill, like Mary Warren, had had a fleeting glimpse of reality. When her master was accused, she saw that the wicked games the girls played had gone too far. She tried to discredit their testimony and in retribution they turned upon her, accusing her of having signed the devil's book. Her brief stand against them collapsed. She, too, confessed that she had signed. Later she would recant her confession before the magistrates, but they would not believe her. After all, who could believe a witch? Still haunted by her false confession, she went in tears to a friend, crying that she had undone herself. She complained that "If she told mr Noys [Reverend Nicholas Noyes of Salem] but ons she had sat hur hand to the Book he would be leve her but If she told the truth and saied she had not seat her hand to the Book a hundred times he would not beleve hur." The incident, however, did not undermine her position as an accuser. She went right along giving testimony to the magistrates against the unlucky persons hauled into court to answer the girls' charges.

Margaret Jacobs, young and impressionable, stood no chance before the girls' demonic onslaught. She quickly confessed herself a witch. For a short time she even became one of the accusers and gave evidence that Burroughs and her grandfather were both wizards. Then her sanity returned. She retracted her confession. She wrote from prison that she had confessed only to save her life and escape hanging. Even that fate seemed better than living each day knowing that her testimony had sent innocent men to the gallows.

The Trials Begin

Throughout May, the jails in Boston and Essex County continued to fill with persons suspected of practicing witchcraft. The legal machinery to bring them to trial did not yet exist. In 1692, the people of Massachusetts were still resolving a governmental problem which had persisted for eight years. In 1684, English courts had revoked the province's original charter, which specified the rights and powers granted to the government, replacing it with one which restricted the colony's independence. With the new charter came Massachusetts's first royal governor, Sir Edmund Andros. His high-handed methods of governing alienated many people. So in 1689, when word reached the colony that William of Orange had overthrown James II in England, a popular uprising in Massachusetts deposed Andros as well. In throwing off the yoke of its royal governor, Massachusetts had lost the authority to establish courts necessary to try capital cases. Until a new charter arrived, the accused witches would remain in prison.

The Reverend Increase Mather (Site 40a; Plate 5), President of Harvard College and father of Cotton Mather, was the province's representative at the English court. He had been in England since 1688 with the sole purpose of obtaining a new charter for Massachusetts. On 14 May 1692, he finally arrived in Boston harbor aboard the ship *Nonesuch*. He brought with him not only the new charter but the new royal governor, Sir William Phips.

Phips was a native New Englander. Though born into a modest family, he had made his fortune by raising a sunken Spanish galleon in the Caribbean. With his share of the profits he also received a knighthood from the Crown. Sir William had returned as governor intent upon defeating the French and Indians, who intermittently attacked the settlements on the frontier. He had not expected to come home to find the prisons full of accused witches. Phips knew that he was not one to lead a crusade against the forces of Satan. He left those matters to his new lieutenant governor, William Stoughton, and to the ministers of the churches, who would know better than he how to deal with these witches. He would see to the French and Indians. Phips never doubted the existence of witches for an instant: as a seventeenth-century mariner, he had heard wondrous tales of the devil and his sea monsters. When Sir William learned that the witch shapes of some now imprisoned still flew about the countryside afflicting the girls, he ordered chains made for the prisoners. The irons supposedly prevented the specter from leaving the witch's body. Some jailers, out of pity, permitted their prisoners to remove their shackles. The girls, who thought that these witches were still in chains, stopped crying out that their specters roamed the land.

The chaining had been only a stopgap measure. Stoughton and the members of the governor's council pressed Phips to appoint a Court of Oyer and Terminer (meaning literally, "to hear and determine") to try the witchcraft cases. Late in May, Phips acquiesced, naming nine men to the special court. William Stoughton was appointed chief justice. The remaining eight justices "were persons of the best prudence and figure that could then be pitched upon," as Phips later wrote. They were Bartholomew Gedney (Site 16b; Plate 22), Jonathan Corwin, John Hathorne, Nathaniel Saltonstall (Site 35; Plate 23), Peter Sergeant, Wait Still Winthrop (Site 38a; Plate 24), Samuel Sewall, and John Richards, some of the most respected men in the province. All were members of the governor's council, but none had had any formal legal training. Richards, Sewall, Winthrop, and Sergeant were from Boston; Saltonstall was from Haverhill; and

(Plate 22; Site 16b) Tomb of Bartholomew Gedney, Salem.

Gedney, Hathorne, and Corwin were from Salem. Stoughton, Sewall, and the Salem justices had already taken active roles in the previous examinations. Over half the court, then, had participated in the witch hunt and could not be expected to be unbiased. Having placed prosecution of the witches in other hands, Phips rode out with an army to the frontier to fight the Indians, an enemy far more tangible than Satan's legions.

A court had at last been established to bring the witches to justice. But the witches in Essex County did not seem overly concerned. Throughout May the number of persons examined and imprisoned on the girls' accusations increased at an alarming rate. By the end of the month approximately one hundred people had been jailed on accusations of witchcraft. Most of their examinations were typical, but three are noteworthy because they illustrate both the girls' machinations and the unconquerable Puritan spirit.

Elizabeth Cary of Charlestown had heard that the girls cried out against her. Of her own accord and accompanied by her

(Plate 23; Site 35)
Tomb of Nathaniel
Saltonstall, Haverhill.

husband, she went to Salem Village to speak with those who had accused her and thereby clear her name. The Carys arrived on May 24, while Hathorne and Corwin were busy examining an accused witch in the Village meetinghouse. The Carys attended this examination and learned the tricks of the girls' trade.

(Plate 24; Site 38a) Tomb of the Winthrop Family, Boston.

The girls lay convulsing on the floor. They were then picked up by the constables, carried over to the accused witch and instructed to touch her. When they did so, their fits ceased. The act of touching, the magistrates said, recalled the witch's torturing specter back to her body. Throughout this entire examination, no girl complained of Mrs. Cary, though she sat before them the whole time. They had already accused her of being a witch, but that accusation had been in name only. No doubt some prompter had suggested to the girls that Cary was a witch and the girls, ever eager for the names of new suspects, had taken up the cry. Still, they had never seen the woman and could not identify her.

The identification was not long in coming. The girls had a malicious habit of asking the names of visitors who came to witness the examinations. When they learned that Mrs. Cary was present, they tumbled to the ground, crying that she afflicted them. She was quickly arrested and brought before the magistrates. The stress of the examination overwhelmed her and, nearly swooning, she begged permission to lean on her husband for bodily support. Hathorne denied her request. "She had strength enough to torment those persons [the girls]," he told her, "and she should have strength enough to stand." When John Indian lay convulsing at her feet, his hand was taken and guided to touch hers. He was miraculously cured, proving that she was a witch. She was imprisoned in Cambridge and, in accordance with the governor's decree, was placed in leg irons weighing eight pounds. Later, at her husband's urging, she escaped to New York. Good people were no longer safe in Massachusetts.

John Alden of Boston was accused on May 28. Stoughton himself personally requested that Alden appear before the magistrates in Salem Village, for he was no ordinary witch. He was the son of John and Priscilla Alden, members of the original Plymouth colony. A sea captain by profession, he had earned the admiration of many people in the province. But in Salem Village, where the girls held power, that counted for little. Hathorne, Corwin, and Gedney examined him on May 31. When the girls fell into fits, the magistrates asked them who caused their torments. One of them hesitatingly pointed a finger at a Captain Hill, who had nothing to do with witchcraft. A man standing behind her stooped down and whispered in her ear. The girl redirected her finger, crying that Alden was the witch. The magistrates asked her how she knew the accused was Alden since she had never seen the man before. She replied that the man behind her had told her so.

Gedney was particularly astonished. For many years he had been Alden's good friend and had believed him an honest man. Now that he saw Alden working witchcraft on the girls he had reason to change his opinion. He urged Alden to confess, but Alden refused; he knew that God would exonerate him. The magistrates ordered him to look at the girls. When he did so they were knocked to the ground. Infuriated, Alden asked why his stare did not knock the magistrates down as well. It was a good question; but the magistrates had no answer and needed none. With their own eyes they had seen Alden torment the girls. Before he was led away, Alden shouted one final truth. If the girls were bewitched, he said, then they were possessed by a "lying Spirit." Nicholas Noyes, minister of Salem, ended the examination with a long prayer which drowned out Alden's further protests.

Martha Carrier of Andover was examined on the same day as Alden. She was, without question, a most defiant witch. When the girls fell into fits, she denied having any hand in it. The black-robed magistrates did not believe her. "What black man did you see?" they asked her, referring to her supposed compact with the devil. "I saw no black man but your own presence," she replied with a sneer. By now the girls' accusations had become outrageous. Carrier had murdered thirteen people in Andover, they said, and the ghosts had come to the meetinghouse to accuse her themselves. "Do not you see them?" they asked the woman. "You lye, I am wronged," Martha answered. Turning to the magistrates, she reproved them for believing the girls' stories. "It is a shamefull thing that you should mind these folks that are out of their wits," she said. The more she denied the accusation, the more hideous the girls' agonies became. Some present thought that the girls would die at any moment. The woman was taken away, her hands and feet tied to prevent her specter from hurting the girls. When she was thus restrained, the girls' fits ended. A witch in bondage could harm no one.

On Thursday, June 2, the Court of Oyer and Terminer held its first session in the courthouse in Salem (Site 14; Plate 25). Good people had awaited the trials with great expectations. After three months of examinations these witches would finally be brought to justice. And if they were condemned they would be executed. "Thou shalt not suffer a witch to live," the Bible commanded. Though there were heated debates concerning how to prove the charge of witchcraft, there was no argument about the penalty once guilt was established. In 1692, witchcraft was a capital offense.

The accused looked to the trials for their vindication. They knew that they had been wrongly accused. With nine of the best minds in Massachusetts sitting in judgment, the girls' outcries would be dismissed and the accused freed. Those accused had

NEARLY OPPOSITE THIS SPOT
STOOD, IN THE MIDDLE OF THE STREET
A BUILDING DEVOTED, FROM 1677 UNTIL 1718,
TO MUNICIPAL AND JUDICIAL USES.
IN IT, IN 1692,
WERE TRIED AND CONDEMNED FOR WITCHCRAFT
MOST OF THE NINETEEN PERSONS
WHO SUFFERED DEATH ON THE GALLOWS.
GILES COREY WAS HERE PUT TO TRIAL
ON THE SAME CHARGE, AND REFUSING TO PLEAD,
WAS TAKEN AWAY AND PRESSED TO DEATH.
IN JANUARY, 1693, TWENTY ONE PERSONS
WERE TRIED HERE FOR WITCHCRAFT,
OF WHOM EIGHTEEN WERE ACQUITTED AND
THREE CONDEMNED, BUT LATER SET FREE,
TOGETHER WITH ABOUT 150 ACCUSED PERSONS,
IN A GENERAL DELIVERY WHICH OCCURRED IN MAY.

(Plate 25; Site 14)
Site of the Courthouse
in 1692, Salem.

been in prison for too long; they had withstood the cruelties of their jailers, the meager prison fare, and the ridicule of pass-ersby. If nothing else, the trials would give them a change from dreary prison life. Hopefully, they would set them free.

Bridget Bishop was the only witch tried on June 2. At her trial, the girls again related how Bishop's specter had tormented them and had brought them the book. Men deposed that Brid-get's shape had appeared to them in the night and had climbed into bed with them. John and William Bly testified that they had found witch dolls made of rags within the cellar wall of Brid-get's Salem house. The dolls had been stuck repeatedly with headless pins. The sum evidence against Bridget, then, was the girls' spectral tales and the fanciful dreams of the townspeople who, through their years of malicious gossip about the woman, had collected enough strange coincidences to suppose her a witch. She had entered a plea of innocent, but on this evidence the court found her guilty. The verdict came as no surprise. Cotton Mather, writing later concerning her case, noted that

"There was little Occasion to prove the Witchcraft, it being Evident and Notorious to all Beholders."

On June 8, William Stoughton signed her death warrant. Two days later, George Corwin (Site 22; Plate 9), High Sheriff of Essex County, took "Brigett Bishop of their Majes'ts Goale in Salem and Safely Conveighd her to the place provided for her Execution and Caused the s'd Brigett to be hanged by the neck untill Shee was dead." Her body was unceremoniously placed in a shallow grave on Gallows Hill (Site 23; Plate 26). Condemned witches did not deserve Christian burial. They were in death as they had been in life: apart from God's chosen people.

That Bridget had been so speedily condemned and executed sent shudders through the rest of the accused. Apparently the court would believe them no more than had the examining magistrates. Yet there was one glimmer of hope. Nathaniel Saltonstall, one of the nine justices, resigned from the court shortly after Bridget was condemned. He had been exceedingly dissatisfied with the blind acceptance of the girls' spectral evidence as proof of witchcraft. He had also disliked the haste with which Stoughton ordered Bridget dispatched to the gallows. Salton-

(Plate 26; Site 23) Gallows Hill, Salem.

stall would become a vocal opponent of the witchcraft proceedings and in time would be accused of witchcraft himself.

Saltonstall's departure from the Court of Oyer and Terminer reflected a division among the justices concerning the type of evidence sufficient to convict a person of witchcraft. At the center of this division stood the spectral evidence. It, more than any other testimony, had sent Bridget Bishop to the gallows. Without spectral evidence there could be no airtight case against the accused. Only arguments between neighbors, strange coincidences, and the personal aberrations of the accused would remain, hardly sufficient evidence to warrant penalty of death.

In June 1692, few people doubted that the girls actually saw the specters that caused their afflictions. The real debate focused on whether a righteous God could permit the devil to afflict the girls in the shape of an innocent person. "He that appeared in the shape of Samuel, a Glorify'd Saint, may Appear in any ones shape," Susannah Martin had argued at her examination in May. The justices, who had diligently searched the Bible for God's revelations on witchcraft, were well aware of the story of the Witch of Endor who had conjured up the spirit of God's servant Samuel.

It was a matter of interpretation whether this story taught the devil's ability or inability to impersonate innocents. Its interpretation, however, was of grave consequence to the magistrates. If the devil could not assume the shape of an innocent person, spectral evidence was invaluable; it alone could convict every witch whose shape the girls had seen. If the devil could appear in the shape of guiltless people, however, the King's Attorney, who would prosecute those accused, had no case against the witches.

The question was inherently theological, so the court turned to the ministers of the colony for an answer. On June 15, five days after Bishop's execution, the ministers submitted a written reply to the justices' request. In it, they thanked the magistrates for their energies in discovering witchcraft. But they advised caution in the upcoming trials "lest by too much credulity for things received only upon the Devil's authority there be a door

opened for a long train of miserable consequences." They coun-
seled that evidence for conviction should be "more considerable
than barely the accused person being represented by a spectre
unto the afflicted" and that the devil could, indeed, assume the
shapes of "virtuous" men to afflict his victims. The importance
of spectral evidence was thus diminished. The tests of "falling at
the sight"—in which a glance from the witch knocked her victims to the ground—and that of touch—in which an afflicted
person could be recalled from a "fitt" by a mere touch from her
tormentor—were both deemed fallible as proof of guilt. All
this advice to exercise caution notwithstanding, the document
closed with an exhortation to the justices recommending "the
speedy and vigorous prosecution of such as have rendered
themselves obnoxious" to the colony.

On June 28, the court reconvened in Salem and resumed
hearing the backlog of cases. It soon became apparent that the
justices had disregarded the ministers' advice to use spectral evidence cautiously, let alone not to rely upon it as the sole basis for
conviction. The chief justice, William Stoughton, rejected outright the possibility of the devil assuming an innocent person's
shape. A just God, he reasoned, would not permit His earthly
servants to be thus deceived. Stoughton had had as much theological training as any minister in Massachusetts and he would
abide by his own convictions. Throughout the entire witchcraft episode he would equate spectral evidence with proof of
witchcraft.

Although the chief justice possessed great influence on the
court, a jury was still responsible for delivering a verdict after
hearing all the evidence. The judicial process of trying the
witches began with a jury of inquest—or grand jury—which
reviewed old evidence and recorded any new testimony in the
case. If the total evidence was sufficient to warrant trial, the accused would be indicted. The case then proceeded to trial before
the Court of Oyer and Terminer. The King's Attorney, Mr.
Thomas Newton (Site 38c), would prosecute the case before a
second jury which consisted entirely of male church members.
This jury heard the evidence gathered by the jury of inquest,

principally the depositions of witnesses for or against the accused. These witnesses would stand before the court, have transcripts of their prior testimony read back to them, and swear to
its truthfulness. Afterward, the jury arrived at a verdict; if
guilty, the justices passed the invariable sentence of death. This
streamlined method of trial permitted the court to prosecute
several cases in one day.

On June 29, Susannah Martin, Sarah Good, and Rebecca
Nurse were tried by the court, convicted, and condemned. At
Martin's trial, in addition to the record of her tormenting the
girls on the day of her examination, others were present to testify. Sarah Atkinson of Newbury stated that Susannah had once
come all the way from her home in Amesbury to Newbury in a
torrential downpour, but had remained completely dry right
down to the soles of her shoes. John Allen of Salisbury testified
that Susannah had bewitched his cattle so that they raced out
into the sea and drowned. The strangest testimony against her
came from one Joseph Ring who claimed to have been transported frequently by various demons to witch meetings during
the previous two years. Ring claimed that these demons had
struck him dumb so he could not speak out against them; now,
with the witch Martin brought to justice, he had regained his
voice and could swear to having seen her at many of the witch
meetings. In her defense Susannah steadfastly maintained that
she "had Led a most virtuous and Holy Life."

At Sarah Good's trial, one of the afflicted girls had a terrible
fit in the courtroom. Upon recovering she cried that Good's
specter had thrust a knife at her breast but that she had evaded
the blow. She grappled with the specter and wrested away the
top half of the knife blade which she held up for all to see. A
young man in attendance, however, objected. He had broken
his knife blade just the other day, he said, in the presence of this
very girl, and had cast away the knife's top half. As proof he
displayed the remaining piece. The justices admonished the girl
not to lie, but permitted her to continue testifying against the
accused.

At Rebecca Nurse's trial the unprecedented occurred. The

jury delivered a verdict of not guilty. At this, the height of the hysteria, her exemplary life and the testimony of her family and friends had outweighed even the tide of evidence from the afflicted girls and the vindictive tales of Sarah Holten and Ann Putnam, Sr. When the girls learned of the decision, they flew into a frenzy of affliction, crying that Nurse's specter tormented them anew. The spectators and members of the court were amazed. One justice expressed himself dissatisfied with the verdict; another, rising to leave, vowed to have her indicted again.

It was William Stoughton who upheld the accusers and tightened the noose around Rebecca's neck. With the courtroom in an uproar, he calmly turned to the jury and asked if they had given sufficient consideration to a statement Rebecca had made during her trial. When Deliverance and Abigail Hobbs, two confessed witches who had been imprisoned with Rebecca, had been brought into the courtroom to give testimony against her, Rebecca had asked, "What, do these persons give in Evidence against me now, they used to come among us," implying that she had once associated with proven witches. This, together with the renewed outcries of the afflicted, compelled the jury to retire and reconsider its verdict.

The jurors, however, were unable to reach a verdict. They disagreed over the meaning of Rebecca's statement. To settle the issue, they filed back into court to ask her themselves. The poor defendant, seated amidst the pandemonium in the courtroom and partially deaf from her advanced age, did not hear their request for an explanation. The foreman of the jury, Thomas Fisk, later wrote that she "made no reply, nor interpretation of them [her earlier remark]; whereupon these words were to me a principal Evidence against her."

When the jury returned the second time they found her guilty and she was carted off to prison to await execution. Upon learning of the jury's interpretation of her remark in court, Rebecca addressed an explanation of its meaning to the justices. Because the Hobbses had been imprisoned with her, she wrote, she did "judge them not legal Evidence against their fellow Prisoners." They therefore could not testify against her. This was the substance of her remark, but the explanation came too late: the court had already condemned her to death. On July 3, Reverend Nicholas Noyes had the woman brought to the meetinghouse in Salem and excommunicated her before the entire congregation. In Puritan theology, excommunication was tantamount to consigning a soul to the fires of hell.

Still, Rebecca's friends fought to save her from the gallows. They petitioned Governor Phips to issue a reprieve of her sentence. He granted their request and Rebecca was temporarily safe. When the afflicted heard of the governor's action, however, they resumed their cries against her with such force and conviction that several gentlemen of Salem prevailed upon the governor to rescind his reprieve. Now nothing stood between Rebecca and execution.

On June 30, two other witches, Sarah Wilds and Elizabeth How of Topsfield, were also tried and condemned. Elizabeth How had been arrested on May 29 and examined before Hathorne and Corwin two days later at Ingersoll's ordinary in Salem Village. Besides perpetrating the usual torments on the girls, How had cured John Indian's fits by a simple touch of her hand. Her specter, however, was more malicious. It had stuck a needle (Site 20) straight into young Ann Putnam's hand. At How's trial, Samuel Perley testified that she had bewitched his daughter. The poor girl had been "struck down, whenever How were spoken of," he said, and "often endeavoured to be Thrown into the Fire, and into the Water, in her strange Fits." Nehemiah Abbot claimed that whenever he had had an altercation with How, strange accidents would befall his cattle; one ox that she cursed had died choking on a turnip. Several confessed witches claimed that she was with them the day they were "baptized by the Devil in the River at Newbery-Falls: before which, he [the devil] made them there kneel down by the Brink of the River and Worship him." Though many of her friends came forward to attest to her Christian life, the woman was beyond acquittal.

At the trials in late June, one of the afflicted had had the temerity to accuse Reverend Samuel Willard of witchcraft. Willard was the respected minister of the Old South Meeting

House in Boston. Three justices of the court were members of
his congregation. The court reprimanded the accuser severely
and sent her from the room. To witnesses they explained that
she had been mistaken: she had meant to accuse John Willard of
Salem Village, they said, who had already been arrested. It is
odd justice when magistrates protect their friends from accusation, yet pursue with a vengeance others accused of the very
same crime.

On Tuesday, July 19, Rebecca Nurse, Elizabeth How, Sarah
Good, Sarah Wilds, and Susannah Martin were taken out of
Salem jail, placed in a cart, and transported through the streets
of the town (Site 19) to Gallows Hill. There Reverend Noyes
urged Sarah Good to confess. He told her that "she was a
Witch, and she knew she was a Witch." Good, defiant to the
end, rebuked him. "You are a lyer," she yelled. "I am no more a
Witch than you are a Wizard, and if you take away my Life,
God will give you Blood to drink." Tradition has it that in 1717,
Noyes succumbed to an internal hemorrhage and died choking
on his own blood.

What the others said before their deaths has been lost to history. They were hanged, cut down, and buried on the hill. That
night members of Rebecca's family returned, removed her body
from its shallow grave, carried it to the Nurse farm, and buried
it secretly in an unmarked grave.

Although the trials were finally underway in earnest, the important task of ferreting out witches still continued unabated.
The accusing circle was equal to the task before it. Throughout
June and into early July, the prisons in Essex County and Boston continued to fill with new witches whose specters the girls
had seen plaguing the countryside.

The Witch Hunt Spreads to Andover

Sometime between the June trials and the July executions, the
witch hunt spilled over into neighboring Andover which, save
for the fiery Martha Carrier, had thus far remained opaque to

the girls' spectral sight. It began with Joseph Ballard, whose wife had been seriously ill for several months. Ballard was no fool. If witchcraft could cause such horrible afflictions in Salem Village, he reasoned, then it might underlie his wife's malady as well. Accordingly he sent to Salem Village to fetch some of the gifted girls who could peer into the invisible world. Others in Andover followed suit. After all, Ballard's wife was not the only sickly person in Andover. The more accusers they could obtain, the faster they would discover Andover's witches.

The authorities in Salem Village dispatched Ann Putnam, Jr. and Mary Walcott to attend to matters in Andover. Upon arrival, the girls were taken to the sick and stationed by their bedsides, one at the patient's head, the other nearer the feet. The girls then used their spectral sight to identify the malefactors who caused the illness. There was, however, a serious problem with the identification of witches in Andover. Neither Ann nor Mary was familiar with the names of the people whose specters they saw. They saw many witches but could name none. To rectify this oversight, the authorities arranged for all those persons suspected of witchcraft to appear before the afflicted girls at the Andover meetinghouse. Reverend Thomas Barnard (Site 34b; Plate 27), the associate minister of Andover's church, opened the examinations with a prayer. The accused were blindfolded and led one by one up to the afflicted girls. It was evidence of witchcraft if the latter went into convulsions when the accused approached them. The "touch" test was applied next. A touch from the supposed witch, which terminated the fit by recalling the tormenting specter back to its master's body, proved witchcraft. No one was quite prepared for what happened that day. Almost every person led before the girls sent them into convulsions and then cured them by touch. Who would ever have suspected Andover of harboring so many witches?

Most of those exposed as witches in Andover were law-abiding men and women who until now had believed very strongly in the witchcraft proceedings. But to find themselves charged with the same crime was unthinkable. Some, fearing the gallows, confessed quickly and told of late-night rides through the air on poles or of witch meetings. Others, made of stronger stuff, initially professed themselves innocent; but their families and friends, who believed the accusations, cajoled, browbeat, and pleaded with their loved ones to confess. They must be witches; the accusing girls, those oracles against the devil, had said so. Martha Tyler, one of those arrested in Andover, related how "her brother kept telling her that she must needs be a witch, since the afflicted accused her, and at her touch were raised out of their fits, and urging her to confess herself a witch." Besides, the court in Salem had to this point tried and condemned only witches who refused to confess. Repentant witches who were contrite for their deviation from Christ's path were temporarily spared from the gallows. They needed time to obtain God's forgiveness for their great sin. For these reasons, many of those accused in Andover confessed to witchcraft. It is ironic that not one person who confessed to witchcraft in 1692 was executed.

Wherever the afflicted girls traveled in Andover, some near them would fall into convulsions and, upon recovery, claim that they, too, had acquired the spectral sight. The number of new accusers in Andover thus increased daily. The most prominent of these was Timothy Swan (Site 34a; Plate 28), a sickly thirty year old who had contracted a fatal disease. In 1692, malefic witchcraft practiced upon him was presumed the sole cause of his illness. Many of the indictments against the Andover witches charged the accused with, among other things, having "tortured, afflicted, tormented, consumed, pined and wasted" the body of Timothy Swan. When the witchcraft hysteria declined late in 1692, Swan's affliction persisted. He would die in February 1693 without any help from the infernal powers.

Now, in July 1692, with fresh accusations coming continually from the girls, the latest converts to the accusing circle, and the newly confessing witches, the number of accused in Andover grew to staggering proportions. Within weeks after Ann Putnam, Jr.'s and Mary Walcott's arrival, over fifty people had been accused and arrested. Andover's justice of the peace, Dudley Bradstreet, son of the colony's former governor, became so dis-

(Plate 27; Site 34b) Grave of Reverend Thomas Barnard, North Andover.

gusted with arrests based on spectral evidence that he refused to issue any more arrest warrants on such tenuous evidence. Shortly afterward, the accusers charged him and his wife with the murders of nine people by witchcraft. Justice Bradstreet lost no time in taking his wife and fleeing Massachusetts Bay. "Poor Andover does now rue the day that ever the said afflicted went among them," wrote Thomas Brattle (Site 38b; Plate 29), an ardent opponent of the witch hunt. "They lament their folly, and are an object of great pity and commiseration."

Even an Andover dog became embroiled in the contagion. The accusers claimed the dog was a witch, and its gaze sent them into convulsions. The dog was put to death. Another dog was said to have been bewitched by the wizard John Bradstreet,

(Plate 28; Site 34a) Grave of Timothy Swan, North Andover.

(Plate 29; Site 38b) Tomb of Thomas Brattle, Boston.

Dudley's brother. Bradstreet fled into New Hampshire to escape the authorities, and this dog was also put to death. It has the dubious distinction of being the only afflicted creature killed during the entire hysteria.

By now the accusers had become heady with their success and it brought the Andover witch hunt to a conclusion almost as rapidly as it had begun. They accused "A worthy Gentleman of Boston" of witchcraft. Instead of appearing before the magistrates to answer to the accusation, or of reasoning with his accusers to prove he was no witch as others had done before to no avail, this "worthy Gentleman" employed a new tactic. He sent friends out from Boston with a warrant to arrest those who had accused him, charging them with slander. The amount of damages sought was £1000, fifty times the average laborer's annual wages. The accusers, who apparently had no qualms about sending innocent persons to prison or to their deaths, balked at the thought of paying £1000 damages. Although no accuser was ever brought to trial to answer the slander charge, from that time forth the accusing voices in Andover faded away. Even so, the damage had been done. Fifty of Andover's inhabitants, some of them her most respected citizens, had been accused and imprisoned. Andover had had a very costly flirtation with the devil.

The Court Reconvenes

On August 2 and the days following, the court again sat in Salem and tried six more witches: Elizabeth and John Proctor, John Willard, George Burroughs, George Jacobs, Sr., and Martha Carrier. Though each pleaded not guilty to the indictment for witchcraft, the court found them all guilty and sentenced them to death. Elizabeth Proctor, who was pregnant, received a stay of execution. The justices would not kill an unborn child even if its parents were a wizard and a witch. After Elizabeth delivered, she would be duly executed. The delay, however, would save her life.

The court tried Martha Carrier on August 2. Several confessing Andover witches testified that she had made them witches and had attended witch meetings in Salem Village with them. One of these witches, Ann Foster, declared that she and Carrier had once ridden to a meeting upon a pole with the devil himself. While in transit, the pole broke and she and Carrier tumbled to the ground. Ann had yet to recover from the injuries she had sustained from the fall. Two men came forward to testify that Martha had afflicted them with sores that never healed. One had a boil on his side which, when lanced, produced "several Gallons of Corruption." The other spoke of having had an old war wound into which a knitting needle would pass four inches. After Martha's arrest, they said, their wounds miraculously disappeared.

Before the entire court, Martha's own sons confessed that she had made them witches and was one herself. Their confessions, however, had been obtained earlier under duress. Carrier's sons "would not confess any thing," John Proctor wrote from prison, "till they [the authorities] tyed them Neck and Heels till the Blood was ready to come out of their Noses." After such torture, they confessed having been witches for one month. They had converted after their mother had already been languishing in prison for three weeks as an accused witch. Although Proctor's writing was not introduced as evidence in court, had it been it would not have saved her. She was a "Rampant Hag," Cotton Mather wrote, and deserved her sentence. "The Devil had promised her, she should be Queen of Hell."

Even from inside prison, John Proctor had struggled against the hysteria. On July 23, he addressed a petition to five ministers from the Boston area known to be opposed to the proceedings in Salem. The judges and juries, he wrote, had "Condemned us already before our Tryals, being so much incensed and engaged against us by the Devil." He had had time to talk with his fellow prisoners. "We know in our own Consciences," he continued, "we are all Innocent Persons." Proctor implored the ministers to use their influence to have the trials moved to Boston or, failing that, to have the justices replaced with more merciful men.

His appeal failed. He stood trial in Salem before the same steely men who had sent five women to the gallows only two weeks before. Most of the testimony against him centered on the crimes his specter had committed during his examination on April 11. Sarah Bibber, for good measure, deposed that on June 3 Proctor's shape had appeared to her and "did most greviously torment me by pinching, pricking and almost presing me to death urging me to drink drink as Red as blood." Mary Warren, Proctor's maidservant, who had once exposed the girls' antics on his behalf, now swore that his specter had forced her to sign the devil's book.

Despite the evidence against him, thirty-one of Proctor's former neighbors in Ipswich braved the vengeance of the accusers and signed a petition in his defense. "His Breading [breeding] hath been Amongst us; and was of Religious Parents in o'r place; & . . . hath had Constant Intercourse w'th us," they wrote. His shape had appeared as a tormentor, they argued, only because God "may p'rmitt Sathan to p'rsonate, Dissemble, & thereby abuse Inocents, & such as Do in the fear of God Defie the Devill and all his works." William Stoughton, who would maintain to the end that an innocent person could not appear as a witch shape, would have none of such reasoning. Proctor was condemned like the rest.

John Willard's trial was an open and shut case. Susannah

Sheldon stated that his specter boasted to her once of having been a wizard for twenty years and had knelt in prayer to a black man wearing a long, crowned hat. Willard's shape was also a murderer. His victims' ghosts, wrapped in their burial shrouds, had appeared to Ann Putnam, Sr. to accuse him, crying for vengeance. His specter had even tortured his own grandfather for having prayed that the kingdom of Satan be overthrown. When Willard was first accused, he had fled to Lancaster to escape arrest. This alone was sufficient to condemn him. "You were fled from Authority," the magistrates had told him at his examination in May. "That is an acknowledgment of guilt." The jury agreed and found him guilty.

On August 5, George Burroughs was brought into court. He was by far the most notorious of all the witches. Not only was he a former minister of the Church but eight confessing witches had accused him of "being an Head Actor at some of their Hellish Randezvouzes, and one who had the promise of being a King in Satans Kingdom." A large crowd which included the Reverend Increase Mather had come to Salem to see him condemned. Inside the courtroom, bedlam reigned. The bewitched girls, who claimed they were being horribly tortured by Burroughs's apparition, testified against him only with the greatest difficulty. When Stoughton asked Burroughs who he thought hindered the girls from testifying, Burroughs answered that "He supposed it was the Divel." Whereupon Stoughton replied, "How comes the Divel so loathe to have any Testimony born against you?" To all assembled it appeared that Satan wanted no evidence given against the man he had appointed to overthrow the Church.

Amidst the uproar in court, some of the girls cried that Burroughs's specter bit them. They rushed to the justices to exhibit the teeth marks on their arms. The justices ordered Burroughs's teeth examined and, to eliminate bias, those of several other men who sat in court. Only Burroughs's teeth matched the marks on the girls' skin.

Burroughs offered little in his own defense, but he refused to confess. He presented a paper he had written to the jury in which he stated "That there neither are, nor ever were Witches, that having made a compact with the Divel, Can send a Divel to Torment other people at a distance." His arguments, however, seemed implausible in light of the tortures which his own specter had inflicted on his accusers before so many witnesses. Moreover, after examining the document closely, the court discerned that it had been excerpted from Thomas Ady's work, *A Perfect Discovery of Witches*. Burroughs was not only a witch, he was a plagiarist. He was found guilty and condemned. "Had I been one of his Judges," Increase Mather later wrote, "I could not have acquitted him." His sentencing, however, did not stop his specter from proceeding with business as usual. Sarah Wilson would later testify that on the night before his execution, Burroughs's specter had taken leave from his fellow witches exhorting them to "Stand to their faith, & not own any thing."

On August 6, George Jacobs, Sr. was tried and condemned. He had earlier denounced the girls as "bitch witches"; now he paid dearly for his opposition. Mary Warren, Mary Walcott, and sixteen-year-old John DeRich testified that Jacobs's specter had brutally beaten them with his walking canes (Site 17). His apparition had also promised Mercy Lewis "gold and many figne things" if, in return, she signed the devil's book. Sarah Bibber testified that Jacobs's shape was present at Bridget Bishop's execution where it had mercilessly beaten Mary Walcott. Even his granddaughter Margaret, who had confessed to witchcraft at her examination in May, gave testimony that he was a wizard. But Margaret was not one to live a lie. Troubled by her conscience, she recanted her confession one day before her grandfather's execution. "What I said, was altogether false against my grandfather," she wrote the magistrates from prison, "which I did to save my life and to have my liberty." No reasonable court member would honor a petition from one witch written in defense of another. Margaret's retraction had only placed her own life in jeopardy. When the time for her own trial came, she was found to have an abscess in her head and her trial was postponed. Later, she would be acquitted. Her grandfather was not so fortunate.

On August 19, Burroughs, Willard, Jacobs, Carrier, and Proctor were taken from Salem jail, placed in a cart, and hauled through Salem to the summit of Gallows Hill. "All of them said they were innocent, Carrier and all," wrote Samuel Sewall, one of the judges who witnessed the hangings. Instead of confessing, they prayed that theirs would be the last innocent blood shed for witchcraft and that the authorities would discover any authentic witches. They then forgave their accusers for having wrongly condemned them.

Burroughs was one of the first to be executed. Before he was hanged, he spoke of his own innocence to those who had maligned him. He talked so calmly and with such sincerity that listeners began to doubt his guilt. He concluded his address with a letter-perfect recitation of the Lord's Prayer. No witch, the magistrates had declared, could perfectly recite the Lord's Prayer. Yet here a convicted wizard, in fact the leader of all the witches in Essex County, had done so. The accusers cried that the black man had whispered the text in his ear. That argument was senseless; Satan couldn't say the prayer either. Burroughs's speech had such an effect on his audience that "it seemed to some, that the Spectators would hinder the Execution."

After Burroughs was hanged, the Reverend Cotton Mather, who had ridden out from Boston to see this minister-turned-witch executed, addressed the crowd. He told them that Burroughs was no longer an ordained minister. "The Devil," he said, "has often been transformed into an Angel of Light." His remarks quieted the rumblings in the crowd. The executions proceeded. Before his death, John Proctor pleaded with the magistrates to stay his execution. He was not prepared to die, he said. They refused. There was no need to give an unrepentant witch more time to prepare for eternity.

The hangings were over. The bodies were cut down, unceremoniously dumped in a large crevice between the rocks on the hill, and covered with dirt. The burials were done with haste. Burroughs's chin and one hand were left protruding from the ground. Convicted witches did not deserve decent burial.

In September, the judicial machinery accelerated the tempo of condemnation. Six witches were tried on the ninth. On the seventeenth, nine more were brought before the court. All were convicted and sentenced to death. The Court of Oyer and Terminer had yet to acquit anyone. On September 22, eight of those condemned were hauled to Gallows Hill and executed.

The court had finally started bringing the confessing witches to justice. The number of confessors had become so large and the jails so overcrowded that they were now a liability to the witch hunt rather than an asset. Some even doubted the sincerity of their confessions. "We had no experience whether they would stand to their Self-condemning confessions, when they came to dye," wrote Reverend John Hale of Beverly. Of the fifteen witches tried in September, four had earlier confessed and were the first of their lot to be placed on trial. They were Rebecca Eames of Boxford, Mary Lacy and Ann Foster of Andover, and the deranged Abigail Hobbs of Topsfield. They had readily admitted their complicity with the devil at their examinations. Now they were repentant. Although the Puritan authorities were cruel toward unconfessing witches, they treated those who confessed with outright mercy. The judges reprieved these four condemned confessors. Before execution they needed time to obtain God's forgiveness for their heinous crimes.

Three of the fifteen witches had pleaded innocent, been found guilty, and were sentenced to death but escaped the gallows: Abigail Faulkner of Andover, Mary Bradbury of Salisbury, and Dorcas Hoar of Beverly. Faulkner was pregnant. Like Elizabeth Proctor, her execution was deferred. Ninety-three of Mary Bradbury's neighbors had signed a petition on her behalf, but it did not help Mary in Salem. When she was condemned, they took matters into their own hands. They smuggled her out of prison and kept her in hiding until the hysteria was past.

Dorcas Hoar barely evaded the hangman. Since her examination in May, when she denounced the girls as "liars," she had maintained her innocence. On September 21, the day before her scheduled execution, she reversed her plea and confessed. Even then, she almost went to the gallows the following day. At the last moment she persuaded Reverends John Hale and Nicholas

Noyes to intercede for her with the authorities. The ministers petitioned the governor requesting that she be granted a month's stay of execution to "perfect her repentance for the salvation of her soule. . . . unless by her relapse, or afflicting others she shall give grounds to hasten her execution." Her execution was accordingly postponed.

The eight remaining witches were executed on September 22. They were Martha Corey of Salem Village, Mary Easty of Topsfield, Alice Parker and Ann Pudeator of Salem, who had all been tried on the ninth; Margaret Scot of Rowley, Wilmott Redd of Marblehead, Samuel Wardwell and Mary Parker of Andover, who had been condemned on the seventeenth.

Ann Pudeator and Alice Parker had been arrested on May 12. They had languished in prison for four long months before their trials. Pudeator was examined at Beadle's Tavern in Salem on July 2. Her accusers charged her with forcing the guileful Sarah Churchill to sign the devil's book. Mary Warren testified that the woman's shape had appeared to her many times and had pinched her and stuck pins into her body. Her neighbor John Best recalled that his deceased wife, who had always had bruises somewhere on her body, had complained "that Ann pudeater would not Lett her alone untill she had killd her By her often pinching & Bruseing of her." Pudeator, in a petition to the judges, later asserted that "John Best hath been formerly whipt and likewise is rcorded [recorded] for a Lyar." She begged the magistrates that "my life may not be taken away by such false Evidence and wittnesses as these." Her appeals were in vain. The false evidence she protested sent her to the gallows.

During Alice Parker's examination on May 12, the afflicted Mary Warren had been so tormented that "her tongue hung out of her mouth until it was black." Her "tongue would be blacker befor she dyed," Alice told the hysterical girl. Parker's specter also specialized in nautical tragedies. Her accusers testified that she had sunk a boat commanded by Thomas Westgate. All those aboard had perished. She had also drowned a boy swimming in Boston Harbor. Despite the overwhelming evidence against her, she would not confess. "If [I] was as free from other

(Plate 30; Site 32) Ambrose Gale House, Marblehead.

sins as from Witchcrafts," she told Reverend Noyes, "[I] would not ask the Lord mercy." She had no confession to make.

At Wilmott Redd's trial, Mary Walcott, Ann Putnam, Jr., and Elizabeth Hubbard testified that Redd's specter had assailed them at her examination in Salem Village on May 31. Her neighbors in Marblehead, Ambrose Gale (Site 32; Plate 30 and Site 33) and Charity Pitman, gave evidence that five years before they had overheard a sharp altercation between Redd and a Mrs. Syms of Salem, who suspected Redd of having pilfered some fine linen. Mrs. Syms became so incensed that she threatened to travel to Salem and report the theft to Magistrate John Hathorne. Redd defied her to go, and told her that until she went she would suffer severe constipation, after which "Mrs. Syms was taken with the distemper of the dry Belly-ake, and so continued many moneths during her stay in the Towne."

Samuel Wardwell and Mary Parker had been arrested only three weeks before their trials. Parker was accused of having afflicted Timothy Swan and Martha Sprague, both of Andover. She had been examined on September 2 before Gedney, Hathorne, Corwin, and John Higginson, Jr. The magistrates had applied the touch test and found that "she recovered all the afflicted out of their fitts by the touch of their hand." A short time later, poor Mary Warren had "a pin run through her hand and blood runeing out of her mouth." The witch Parker, Warren said, had caused her torments.

Wardwell, at his examination, had been so intimidated by the magistrates that he confessed he was a wizard. Twenty years before, he said, a black man had appeared to him, who called himself "prince and lord" and commanded Wardwell to worship him. In exchange, the man promised that Wardwell "should never want for any thing." Apparently the black man failed to fulfill his obligation. "The black man had never performed any thing," Wardwell lamented. Later, he had signed his name in the devil's book and was baptized into Satan's kingdom in the Shawsheen River. The devil had promised him that they would covenant together until Wardwell was sixty. In 1692, he still had fourteen years to go.

After he confessed, his conscience gave him no rest. On September 13, before the jury of inquest, he recanted his confession. He had given false witness against himself, he said, and was willing to die with a clear conscience. When his previous confession was submitted as evidence, the jury had no difficulty deciding his guilt. Dorcas Hoar, to save her life, had lied; Samuel Wardwell, to save his soul, had recanted.

On September 19, Giles Corey was pressed to death. He had pleaded not guilty to his indictment. But under Old English Law, defendants in felony cases such as witchcraft were also required to "put themselves upon the country": that is, to acknowledge the court's right to try them for their crimes. Until they did so they could not legally be tried. Corey knew that if he were convicted as a witch his property would be forfeited to the Crown. Without a trial, however, he could not be convicted; and without conviction, his property could not be confiscated. The court in Salem had thus far acquitted no one.

While in prison, Corey had taken the precautionary measure of transferring his property to his sons-in-law; but he was still troubled. If he were tried and found guilty, the transferal might be invalidated. He would surrender his life to these witch hunters, he decided, but never his property. He refused to acknowledge the court's right to try him. Without a trial, his property was secure.

The law, however, provided a means for dealing with recalcitrants like Giles Corey who "stood mute" before the court. They came under sentence of *peine forte et dure*, "a punishment hard and severe." He was taken to a Salem field and there staked to the ground. A large wooden plank was placed over him. Upon it were piled stones one at a time. The authorities intended to change his mind with force. Tradition has it that Corey pleaded only for "more weight" so that he might die swiftly. "In pressing," a contemporary wrote, "his Tongue being prest out of his Mouth, the Sheriff [George Corwin] with his Cane forced it in again, when he was dying." His was a horrible death. But young Ann Putnam saw justice in it. Years before, she said, when Corey had made his pact with the devil, the latter promised him that he would never hang. His pact, Ann said, foretold the manner of his death.

Three days later, the seven condemned witches and one lone wizard were carted off to Gallows Hill. As the cart ascended the hill, it stuck in a rut in the dirt path. The accusers shouted that the devil, who sought to prevent the executions, had halted the cart. Strong Puritan hands soon freed it and the procession continued to the summit.

Once there, the condemned addressed the people who had come to see them die. Martha Corey, protesting her innocence to the end, "concluded her Life with an Eminent Prayer." Wardwell's words were cut short by smoke from the executioner's pipe which had wafted into his face. His accusers cried that "the Devil hindred him with smoak" although it did seem odd that Satan would stifle his own servant. Mary Easty's remarks were remembered as having been so "Serious, Religious, Distinct, and Affectionate" that barely a dry eye could be found among those assembled. Reverend Nicholas Noyes, however, shed no tears. After the hangings were over, he turned to the bodies dangling from the tree and said, "What a sad thing it is to see Eight Firebrands of Hell hanging there."

Spectral Evidence Invalidated

None realized that the hangings of September 22 were to be the last executions of the witchcraft hysteria. After all, witches were still being discovered in Massachusetts. The executed Samuel Wardwell and Mary Parker had been arrested only three weeks before their deaths. The court was scheduled to sit again on the first Tuesday in November. With the righteous William Stoughton still presiding, surely more witches would be condemned and executed. Those watching the hangings that day were sure of it.

They were wrong. In October, the forces opposed to the witchcraft trials would rise up and strip them of the crucial evidence which had sent every witch to the gallows. They would invalidate the spectral evidence.

The ministers of the colony led the vanguard of the attack. Except for Hale, Parris, and Noyes, who had played prominent roles in the prosecutions, almost every minister had been in one way or another opposed to the proceedings in Salem. In an address before a convocation of ministers in Cambridge on October 3, Reverend Increase Mather reiterated his belief that spectral evidence should be used only with the greatest caution. "It were better that ten suspected Witches should escape," he told his audience, "than that one innocent Person should be Condemned."

Mather was near the breaking point. Several days before his speech he had reproved a Boston man for taking his sick child to Salem to consult the young seeresses about the identity of the child's tormentors. "[Is] there not a God in Boston," Mather had thundered, "that [you] should go to the Devill in Salem for advice?" This was the same man who had written that had he been one of the judges at George Burroughs's trial, he could not have voted for acquittal. Times had changed.

On October 8, Thomas Brattle, a wealthy Boston merchant, wrote a famous "Letter" attacking the Salem examinations and trials. Although it went unpublished, the letter saw wide circulation among the learned members of the colony. It had a great impact. In it Brattle decisively refuted much of the evidence that had been used to obtain convictions in Salem. Most importantly he debunked the validity of spectral evidence:

> . . . the afflicted do own and assert, and the Justices do grant, that the Devill does inform and tell the afflicted the names of those persons that are thus unknown unto them. Now these two things being duly considered, I think it will appear evident to any one, that the Devill's information is the fundamental testimony that is gone upon in the apprehending of the aforesaid people.

The ministers, the magistrates, and the people of Massachusetts had been deluded by the devil. If Brattle was correct, they had wrongly executed twenty innocent people and imprisoned countless others.

Several days later, Governor Phips became directly involved. From the start he had never liked the court's reliance on spectral evidence. In July he had reprieved Rebecca Nurse. Only the renewed clamor of the afflicted had caused him to revoke his reprieve. Phips had depended on the ministers of the colony and on his lieutenant governor, William Stoughton, to decide the value of spectral evidence. It was an unfortunate choice. Stoughton valued it enough to hang people on its authority alone. In October, Phips took matters into his own hands. In a letter to the Privy Council in London dated October 12, he wrote that he now "found that the Devill had taken upon him the name and shape of severall persons who were doubtless inocent." He ordered that no new witches be imprisoned and postponed the court's proceedings until he received guidance from England. The Court of Oyer and Terminer would meet no more. On October 29, Phips ordered it dissolved.

In November 1692, seventeen-year-old Mary Herrick went

to the Reverends Joseph Gerrish of Wenham (Site 30; Plate 31 and Site 28a; Plate 32) and John Hale of Beverly and told them that the specter of Hale's wife (Site 25) afflicted her. Hale had been a steadfast defender of spectral evidence. He had given testimony against Bridget Bishop and Sarah Wilds, which helped send them both to the gallows. But his own wife, he knew, was a sincere Christian. Even if a specter resembling his wife tormented the girl, she had nothing to do with witchcraft. If his wife was innocent, and of that Hale was certain, then the spectral evidence was fallible; the devil could assume the shape of an innocent person. What did that say, he wondered, about the poor wretches who had already been executed? Surely some of them had been innocent as well.

Mary Herrick told Gerrish and Hale the following tale. On September 22, the same day of her execution, the apparition of that proven witch Mary Easty had appeared to Mary and told her, "I am going upon the Ladder to be hanged for a Witch, but I am innocent, and before a 12 Month be past you shall believe it." But Herrick, convinced that Easty was a witch, told no one.

Since September, other apparitions had come to her and tor-

(Plate 31; Site 30) Claflin-Gerrish-Richards House, Wenham.

(Plate 32; Site 28a) Tomb of Reverend Joseph Gerrish, Wenham.

tured her. She identified Mrs. Hale as her foremost tormentor.
On November 12, Mrs. Hale's shape appeared to her again and
afflicted her. This time it was accompanied by the ghost of
Mary Easty. Easty's spirit had come, it said, "to tell her She had
been put to Death wrongfully and was Innocent of Witchcraft."
It ordered Mary to go and tell Reverends Hale and Gerrish what
had happened. After this, the ghost promised, it "would rise no
more, nor should Mrs. Hayle Afflict her any more." With Mary
Herrick's testimony against his wife, Hale could no longer
believe in the spectral evidence. Herrick, her mission accom-
plished, was never again haunted by the ghost of Mary Easty.

Writing years later, Hale attributed the collapse of the witch
hunt to a growing realization that the affair had gone too far. So
many people had been accused of witchcraft, Hale wrote, that
no one could imagine how "so many in so small a compass of
Land should so abominably leap into the Devils lap at once."
Some of these had led "blameless and holy lives"; except for the
cries of their accusers, no sane man would have suspected many
of them of witchcraft. Hale was also troubled by the ever-

increasing number of accusers. By late 1692, their number had climbed to over fifty people. In a land where witches were being brought to justice, he had expected the number of afflicted to diminish rather than increase. Sadly, he remembered the nineteen who had been executed. Had they all been guilty, he wrote, surely some of them would have sought "Mercy for their Souls in the way of Confession and sorrow for such a Sin." Instead, they had all died unrepentant. Now in 1692, John Hale would no longer participate in shedding innocent blood. He added his voice to those denouncing the witchcraft proceedings.

In early November, Lieutenant James Stephens of Gloucester, like Joseph Ballard before him, sent for some of the accusers. Stephens had learned that his ill sister, Mary Fitch, was a victim of witchcraft. He needed those with spectral vision to identify the culprits. Some of the accusers hurried over to aid in the hunt. While crossing over Ipswich bridge on their way to Gloucester, "they met with an old Woman, and instantly fell into their Fits." So discredited had the spectral evidence become that their folly was ignored. The old woman was permitted to go her way. Gloucester was lucky. Had it been July and not November, Gloucester might have suffered the same fate as Andover.

Although the storm of accusation was past, the prisons in Massachusetts were still bursting with suspects arrested that summer. Eight other women had been condemned and awaited execution. Until these cases were concluded, the colony would live on in the shadow of witchcraft.

On November 25, the General Court of the colony created a Superior Court to try the remaining witchcraft cases and thus empty the prisons. Its members were Lieutenant Governor William Stoughton, again presiding as chief justice, John Richards, Wait Still Winthrop, Samuel Sewall, and Thomas Danforth. To the accused this was disheartening news. Except for Danforth, who had been present at some of the examinations, the men who were to try them were former members of the old Court of Oyer and Terminer, and they had acquitted none. There was a difference, however. After Governor Phips dissolved the court in October, several of the justices came to see him. They "acknowledged that their former proceedings were too violent and not grounded upon a right foundation," Phips later wrote, "but that if they might sit againe, they would proceed after another method." He gave them their second chance.

There were two major differences between the newly appointed Superior Court and the old Court of Oyer and Terminer. First, the trials would no longer be held exclusively in Salem. The court was instead to travel to the county seats to try each accused witch in her own county. Most importantly, spectral evidence would no longer be admissible in court. When one jury inquired of the judges the value of spectral evidence in determining guilt, they were told "as much as of Chips in Wort" (i.e., worthless).

The Superior Court first sat in Salem on 3 January 1693. Without spectral evidence, convictions became the exception rather than the rule. Juries, mindful of the events of the preceding summer, feared convicting even one innocent person. Of fifty-six cases brought before the court in its first session, thirty had insufficient evidence to warrant even indictment. Of the remainder, only three women were found guilty. Two of them, Elizabeth Johnson of Andover and Mary Post of Rowley, were described as "the most senseless and Ignorant Creatures that could be found." The third was Samuel Wardwell's wife, Sarah. She had confessed to witchcraft after her arrest and was therefore condemned. Stoughton speedily signed death warrants for the three women and for five of those condemned in September. The court then adjourned until the end of the month. It would reconvene in Charlestown in Middlesex County.

When Phips heard of the impending executions, he collared the King's Attorney General, Captain Anthony Checkley, who had replaced Thomas Newton on 26 July 1692. Checkley informed the governor that, in his opinion, there was no more evidence against the three who had been condemned than against the fifty-three who had been acquitted. Phips had had enough of executing innocent people. He had also had enough of William Stoughton. The lieutenant governor, he complained to the Privy Council, "hath from the beginning hurried on these matters with great precipitancy and by his warrant hath caused the estates, goods and chattles of the executed to be seized and disposed of without my knowledge or consent." Accordingly, he reprieved the eight condemned witches.

The Superior Court had resumed hearing cases in Charlestown on January 31 when word of the governor's reprieve arrived. Stoughton was so incensed when he learned of Phips's action that he thundered, "We were in a way to have cleared the Land of these [witches]. Who it is obstructs the course of Justice I know not; the Lord be merciful to the Countrey." With that he stormed out of the courtroom. He refused to participate in any more trials while the court still sat in Charlestown.

Of all those tried at Charlestown, the case of Lydia Dustin was the most remarkable. Lydia was an ancient woman and had been considered a witch by many for over thirty years. Before her trial began, her accusers circulated their opinion "that if there were a Witch in the World she was one." A multitude of people gave evidence against her, citing chiefly accidents or illnesses which had occurred after they had argued with her. Without the weapon of spectral evidence, even she was acquitted. Some of those present, who had also attended the trials in Salem the previous summer, told one of the judges "that there was more Evidence against the said Daston [Dustin] than against any at Salem, to which the said Judge conceeded, saying, That it was so." The others tried at Charlestown were also acquitted.

On 25 April 1693, the Superior Court sat in Boston, and William Stoughton was once again in attendance. There it acquitted every person brought to trial. Even a confessing witch, Mary Watkins, who was felt to be mentally ill, was acquitted. The jurors were going to great lengths to avoid condemning the innocent.

The Superior Court sat for the last time on 9 May 1693 in Ipswich to try the remaining witchcraft cases in Essex County. Several people who had been arrested for witchcraft in Andover in 1692 were acquitted. William Barker, Jr. (Site 34d), who had initially confessed himself a witch but now pleaded not guilty to his indictment, was one of them. There were no convictions.

Later that month, Governor Phips ordered that any person still imprisoned on the charge of witchcraft was to be set free. There was a catch, however. In seventeenth-century Massachusetts, prisoners were required to pay for their food and lodging during their imprisonment. Only those who could pay their prison bills or find someone to do so for them were released. Those who could not languished in prison.

Aftermath

The accusations, the examinations, the trials, and the executions at last were at an end. But the memories lingered on. So many people had been involved in the accusations, and so many others accused, that the horrors of 1692 could not be easily forgotten. Some never forgot and never forgave. In 1697, when High Sheriff George Corwin died, Philip English, Salem's wealthiest merchant, seized Corwin's body and demanded partial reimbursement of the £1500 that Corwin had confiscated in the King's name when English stood accused of witchcraft. He forced Corwin's executors to pay him £60 in exchange for the corpse. It was not until 1736, when he was on his deathbed, that English found it in his heart to forgive Magistrate John Hathorne for his judicial excesses in 1692. Even then he forgave with reservations. "If I get well," English threatened, "I'll be damned if I forgive him!"

In 1697, Samuel Parris, in whose parsonage the entire sorry affair had begun, became another of its victims. His parishioners forced him to resign his position as minister in Salem Village. The family of Rebecca Nurse was aroused against him, and had worked for four years to have him ousted. He had, after all, taken a leading role in Rebecca's prosecution. Parris, they wrote in a petition to Wait Still Winthrop, had "been the beginner and procurer of the sorest afflictions [the witchcraft], not to this village only, but to this whole country." In 1696 the minister lost his wife, the good and pious Elizabeth. Although he later remarried, his remaining life was full of sorrow. He died in Sudbury, Massachusetts, in 1720.

The horde of accusers, who had sent so many to prison and the gallows in 1692, faded into history. Tituba, who had blazed the trail for so many others by her confession, recanted her story. She claimed that she had been beaten into confession by her master, Reverend Samuel Parris. "Whatsoever she said by way of confessing or accusing others," she declared, "was the effect of such usage." Others who had followed in her footsteps and confessed generally renounced their confessions. Some swore that they "remembred nothing of what they said; others said they had belied themselves and others," wrote John Hale in 1697. The accusing girls, who, in the end, were ignored and discredited, fell silent. Some, like Mary Walcott and Elizabeth Booth, married and had families. Others disappeared into the darker side of Puritan society. "Some of the Principal Accusers and Witnesses in those dark and severe Prosecutions," reads an act passed by the General Court in 1711, "have since discovered themselves to be Persons of Profligate and Vicious Conversation."

There was one great exception, however. At a church meeting in Salem Village in 1706, Ann Putnam, Jr., who had played such a pivotal role in the accusations and trials, stood before her parishioners and publicly begged forgiveness. The years since 1692 had been harsh for young Ann. Her parents, Thomas and the spiteful Ann, Sr., had died in 1699 within a fortnight of one another, leaving young Ann to care for their large family. The resulting physical strain had been too great for the girl to bear. In 1706 she was sickly and ten short years from her own death. She had been only twelve when the hysteria erupted, but after fourteen years, even she could not discern how it had begun. "What was said or done by me against any person," she explained in 1706, "I can truly and uprightly say, before God and man, I did it not out of any anger, malice, or ill-will to any person, for I had no such thing against one of them; but what I did was ignorantly, being deluded by Satan. . . . I desire to lie in the dust, and earnestly beg forgiveness of God, and from all those unto whom I have given just cause of sorrow and offence."

Young Ann was not the only actor in the Salem tragedy to repent his role in the witch hunt. On 14 January 1697, the colony observed a "Day of Prayer, with Fasting," seeking God's pardon for "all the Errors of his Servants and People, that desire to love his Name," particularly with regard "to the late Tragedy, raised among us by Satan and his Instruments." That day, Samuel Sewall, former justice of the infamous Court of Oyer and Terminer, stood before his congregation in the Old South Meeting House in Boston and heard his confession read to him from the pulpit. Sewall wrote of "the Guilt contracted upon the opening of the late Commission of Oyer and Terminer at Salem" and desired "to take the Blame and shame of it, Asking pardon of men."

That same day, Thomas Fisk and eleven other former jurors who had sat in judgment at Salem (Site 28b; Plate 33 and Site 28c) signed a petition asking forgiveness from those they had wronged. "We confess that we our selves were not capable to understand, nor able to withstand the mysterious delusions of the Powers of Darkness, and Prince of the Air; . . . whereby we fear we have been instrumental with others, tho Ignorantly and unwittingly, to bring upon our selves, and this People of the Lord, the Guilt of Innocent Blood." Almost five years after her examination, Martha Corey's sound reasoning had at last been vindicated. "We must not beleive all that these distracted children say," she had protested. These jurors had had a painful education, but they had learned; and they were strong enough to admit their error. "[We] do declare according to our present minds," they concluded, "we would none of us do such things again on such grounds for the whole World."

And what of William Stoughton, that "most strenuous Opponent of Impiety and Vice," whose signature had sent nineteen people to the gallows? The former chief justice never made a public apology for having hounded the witches in 1692. Indeed, he felt he had done nothing which required absolution. As a justice, he said, he had acted in good faith and to the best of his abilities in the interest of the colony. No man need apologize for that. Tradition has it that he once remarked that even if he had erred in the witchcraft, he would seek God's forgiveness and

(Plate 33; Site 28b) Grave of Thomas Fisk, Jr., Wenham.

not men's. Stoughton continued to serve the colony until his death in 1701.

In 1697, Reverend John Hale examined the Salem hysteria and the evidence used in convicting witches in his short work *A Modest Enquiry into the Nature of Witchcraft*. Hale had long been troubled by the executions in 1692. "I have had a deep sence of the sad consequence of mistakes in matters Capital; and their impossibility of recovering when compleated," he wrote. The men of 1692 meant well and sought God's guidance and direction. "But," he continued, "such was the darkness of that day, the tortures and lamentations of the afflicted, and the power of former presidents, that we walked in the clouds, and could not see our way." In the interim, Massachusetts had learned from its brush with the devil. The old evidence used to prove witchcraft, which was "too slender to evidence the crime they were brought to prove," Hale concluded, could no longer be accepted in any court.

In his "Letter" of October 1692, Thomas Brattle had lamented that the witchcraft would so besmirch Massachusetts that "ages will not wear off that reproach and those stains which these things will leave behind them upon our land." Although the memory of the witch hunt continues to this day, it is significant that within fifteen years of the Salem trials, individuals from each of the groups that had participated in the witch hunt—the accusers, the justices, the jurors, and the clergy—had come forward to acknowledge their errors, ask forgiveness, and amend their ways. The Puritans were a hard and a proud people, but neither hard enough nor proud enough to be blind to their mistakes. In a way, the Salem tragedy represents a triumph of the Puritan spirit. The people had learned. Never again would Massachusetts capitulate its reason to an onslaught from the "Prince of the Air" as it once did in 1692.

Chronology

November 1689: Samuel Parris becomes minister in Salem Village.

Winter months of 1691–92: Tituba holds her clandestine meetings with the Village girls in the parsonage.

1692

January 20: Nine-year-old Elizabeth Parris, the minister's daughter, begins acting strangely. Within days, the other girls of the neighborhood are likewise afflicted.

Mid-February: Dr. William Griggs, physician in Salem Village, states that the girls are bewitched.

Late February: Local ministers pray with the afflicted girls at the Village parsonage in hopes of discovering their tormentors.

Around February 25: On the advice of Mary Sibley, a member of Parris's congregation, Tituba and John Indian bake a witch cake made with rye meal and the girls' urine in an effort to expose the witches.

February 29: Warrants for the arrests of Sarah Good, Sarah Osborne, and Tituba Indian are issued.

March 1: Tituba, Sarah Good, and Sarah Osborne are examined in the meetinghouse in Salem Village by magistrates John Hathorne and Jonathan Corwin. Only Tituba confesses.

March 11: Parris meets with several neighboring ministers at the Village parsonage for "a Solemn day of Prayer" concerning the witchcraft.

March 12: Ann Putnam, Jr. accuses Martha Corey of witchcraft.

March 19: Reverend Deodat Lawson arrives in Salem Village to investigate charges that his deceased wife was murdered by witchcraft. Abigail Williams accuses Rebecca Nurse of witchcraft.

March 21: Martha Corey is examined before Hathorne and Corwin in Salem Village.

March 24: Rebecca Nurse is examined before Hathorne and Corwin in Salem Village.

March 28: John Proctor's wife, Elizabeth, is denounced as a witch.

Early April: Mary Warren, one of the accusing girls, claims that the other girls "dissemble" in their fits.

April 3: Rebecca Nurse's sister, Sarah Cloyce, is accused of witchcraft.

April 11: Elizabeth Proctor and Sarah Cloyce are examined in Salem Town before Hathorne, Corwin, Deputy Governor Thomas Danforth, and Captain Samuel Sewall. During the examination John Proctor is accused and afterward imprisoned.

April 19: Abigail Hobbs, Bridget Bishop, Giles Corey, and Mary Warren are examined in Salem Village. Abigail Hobbs confesses. Mary Warren withdraws her charge that the other girls feigned their convulsions.

April 22: Nehemiah Abbot, William and Deliverance Hobbs, Edward and Sarah Bishop, Mary Easty, Mary Black, Sarah Wilds, and Mary English are examined before Hathorne and Corwin in Salem Village. Only Nehemiah Abbot is cleared by the accusing girls.

May 2: Sarah Morey, Lydia Dustin, Susannah Martin, and Dorcas Hoar are examined by the magistrates in Salem Village.

May 4: George Burroughs is arrested in Wells, Maine.

May 9: Burroughs is examined at Nathaniel Ingersoll's ordinary in Salem Village by Hathorne, Corwin, Sewall, and William Stoughton. Sarah Churchill, one of the afflicted girls, is also examined.

May 10: George Jacobs, Sr. and his granddaughter Margaret are examined at Beadle's Tavern before Hathorne and Corwin.

Margaret confesses and testifies that her grandfather and George Burroughs are both witches.

May 10: Sarah Osborne dies in prison in Boston.

May 14: Increase Mather returns from England aboard the *Nonesuch*, bringing with him the new charter and the new royal governor, Sir William Phips.

May 18: Mary Easty is released from prison. The renewed outcries of her accusers, however, result in her second arrest on May 20.

May 24: Elizabeth Cary of Charlestown visits Salem Village and is accused of witchcraft.

May 27: The Court of Oyer and Terminer is established to try the witchcraft cases. Its members are: Lieutenant Governor William Stoughton, Nathaniel Saltonstall, Bartholomew Gedney, Peter Sergeant, Samuel Sewall, Wait Still Winthrop, John Richards, John Hathorne, and Jonathan Corwin.

May 31: Martha Carrier, John Alden, Wilmott Redd, Elizabeth How, and Philip English are examined in Salem Village before Hathorne, Corwin, and Gedney.

June 2: Bridget Bishop is tried and condemned at the first sitting of the court in Salem.

Sometime after June 2: Nathaniel Saltonstall, dissatisfied with its proceedings, resigns from the court.

June 10: Bridget Bishop is executed on Gallows Hill in Salem.

June 15: Twelve ministers of the colony submit their advice to the court cautioning reliance on spectral evidence to obtain convictions.

June 16: Roger Toothaker of Billerica, who was arrested on May 18, dies in prison in Boston.

June 29–30: Rebecca Nurse, Susannah Martin, Sarah Wilds, Sarah Good, and Elizabeth How are tried and condemned by the court in Salem.

Around July 14: Joseph Ballard of Andover sends to Salem Village to obtain the aid of the accusing girls in exposing the witches afflicting his wife, thus beginning the Andover witch hunt.

July 19: Rebecca Nurse, Susannah Martin, Elizabeth How, Sarah Good, and Sarah Wilds are executed on Gallows Hill.

July 26: Captain Anthony Checkley replaces Thomas Newton as Attorney General of the Court of Oyer and Terminer.

August 2–6: George Jacobs, Martha Carrier, George Burroughs, John and Elizabeth Proctor, and John Willard are tried and condemned. Elizabeth's pregnancy postpones her execution.

August 18: Margaret Jacobs recants her confession.

August 19: George Jacobs, Martha Carrier, George Burroughs, John Proctor, and John Willard are hanged on Gallows Hill. After Burroughs's death, Cotton Mather pacifies the disgruntled crowd "saying, That the Devil has often been transformed into an Angel of Light."

September 9: Martha Corey, Mary Easty, Alice Parker, Ann Pudeator, Dorcas Hoar, and Mary Bradbury are tried and condemned.

September 17: Margaret Scot, Wilmott Redd, Samuel Wardwell, Mary Parker, Abigail Faulkner, Rebecca Eames, Mary Lacy, Ann Foster, and Abigail Hobbs are tried and condemned.

September 19: Giles Corey is pressed to death for refusing to stand trial.

September 21: Dorcas Hoar confesses to witchcraft, the first of those pleading innocent to confess. Her execution is delayed.

September 22: Martha Corey, Margaret Scot, Mary Easty, Alice Parker, Ann Pudeator, Wilmott Redd, Samuel Wardwell, and Mary Parker are hanged on Gallows Hill.

September 22: William Stoughton, John Hathorne, Reverend Cotton Mather, Captain John Higginson, Jr., and Samuel and Stephen Sewall meet in Samuel Sewall's house in Boston. There they discuss publishing an official account of the witch trials. It is later written by Cotton Mather and published under the title *The Wonders of the Invisible World*.

September 22: Just before her execution, the specter of Mary Easty appears to Mary Herrick of Wenham and declares "I am innocent, and before a 12 Month be past you shall believe it."

October 3: Increase Mather addresses a convocation of ministers in Cambridge, warning against placing too great a reliance on spectral evidence.

October 8: Thomas Brattle writes his famous "Letter," sharply criticizing the witchcraft proceedings in Salem.

October 12: Governor Phips informs the Privy Council in London of his having forbidden further imprisonments on the charge of witchcraft.

October 29: Governor Phips dissolves the Court of Oyer and Terminer.

November 14: Mary Herrick tells Reverend John Hale that his wife afflicts her.

November 25: The General Court of the colony creates the Superior Court to try the remaining witchcraft cases. The new court's members are: Lieutenant Governor William Stoughton, Thomas Danforth, John Richards, Wait Still Winthrop, and Samuel Sewall.

December 14: The General Court passes a bill declaring witchcraft a capital offense.

1693

January 3–13: At the first sitting of the new Superior Court in Salem, only three of fifty-six persons accused of witchcraft are condemned. Stoughton speedily signs death warrants for these three and for five others condemned in 1692.

January 31: The Superior Court reconvenes in Charlestown and tries the witch cases in Middlesex County. No convictions are obtained. Stoughton leaves the bench when word arrives that Governor Phips has reprieved the eight he had condemned to death.

February 21: Phips writes his second witchcraft letter to the Privy Council charging that Stoughton "hath from the beginning hurried on these matters with great precipitancy."

March 10: Lydia Dustin dies in prison. She had been acquitted at the January 31 session of the Superior Court but had been unable to pay her prison fees.

April 25: The Superior Court convenes in Boston. John Alden is acquitted by proclamation.

May 9: The Superior Court sits for the last time in Ipswich. William Barker, Jr. of Andover is acquitted.

May: Governor Phips pardons those still imprisoned on the charge of witchcraft.

Sites

This section contains descriptions of the sites from the witch-craft hysteria which can still be seen today. With few exceptions, only original houses or foundations, gravesites, and sites indicated by historic markers have been included. Sites lacking either physical remains or any historic marker have generally been omitted. Except where otherwise noted, all gravesites mentioned are marked. Following each site is a short description of its relevance to the witchcraft events. Each site has been assigned a number which identifies it in both the map and historical sections.

Danvers

Known in 1692 as Salem Village, Danvers was the scene of the outbreak of witchcraft in Essex County. The strange actions of the young girls in the area first began at the parsonage, home of Reverend Samuel Parris. Those first accused of witchcraft lived in Danvers. As the witchcraft contagion spread, however, people throughout all Essex County were accused. Many people accused of witchcraft were examined by the magistrates in the meetinghouse in Danvers. When the Court of Oyer and Terminer was appointed in May 1692, the trials and executions were moved to neighboring Salem, the county seat.

1. Foundations of the 1692 Parsonage (Plate 1; located behind 67 Centre Street). These are the foundations of the Salem

97

Village parsonage where the hysteria began. It was here, in the home of the Reverend Samuel Parris and his wife, Elizabeth, that the circle of girls met in the winter months of 1691–92 to listen to Tituba's tales of magic and the occult. In January 1692, the Parrises' daughter Elizabeth began behaving strangely and was diagnosed as bewitched. In this house Tituba and John Indian baked the witch cake which prompted the accusations, and eleven-year-old Abigail Williams, in full possession, spied the specter of Rebecca Nurse. The parsonage was built by the parish in 1681 for use by its ministers. In it lived Reverend George Burroughs (1681–83) who was hanged as a witch in 1692, Reverend Deodat Lawson (1684–88) who returned to Salem Village in 1692 at the outbreak of the witchcraft, and Reverend Samuel Parris (1689–96). The parsonage was torn down in 1784. Its foundations were excavated in 1970.

2. Nathaniel Ingersoll's Ordinary (Plate 10; 199 Hobart Street, located at the intersection of Hobart and Centre Streets). This building, constructed around 1670, was Deacon Nathaniel Ingersoll's ordinary, one of the most important landmarks of the hysteria. Visitors to the Village in 1692 often sought lodging here; and here the magistrates and marshals of Essex County ate and drank during their recesses from examining accused witches. Reverend Deodat Lawson, a former minister of Salem Village, returned there in March 1692 and, he later wrote, "lodged at Nathaniel Ingersols near to the Minister Mr. P's. [Parris's] house." Nathaniel Cary of Charlestown wrote that he came to the Village with his wife Elizabeth and "went therefore into the Alehouse [Ingersoll's ordinary], where an Indian Man [John Indian, Tituba's husband] attended us, who it seems was one of the afflicted." Moments later, the pack of girls exploded into the room, "began to tumble down like Swine," and accused Elizabeth of witchcraft. A portion of Ingersoll's bill to the colony for his services includes the following: "Upon Examination of Goodwife Corry To the Marshall for Horses

& Drink . . . 6d . . . To the Majestrates Horses; Drink and Entertainment . . . 4s."

Most of those examined for witchcraft in Salem Village were brought to this ordinary and examined later in the Village meetinghouse down the road. It is probable that some examinations were conducted in the ordinary itself. Ingersoll's ordinary is privately owned.

3. Site of the Salem Village Meetinghouse (Plate 11; located at the intersection of Forest and Hobart Streets). The meetinghouse of the First Church in Salem Village stood here in 1692. The meetinghouse was the site of most of the 1692 examinations, although some examinations were held in the Salem meetinghouse, in Beadle's Tavern in Salem, and in Ingersoll's ordinary. Nathaniel Cary, whose wife, Elizabeth, was arrested on May 24, described the meetinghouse in Salem Village as "the place appointed for that Work [i.e., the examinations]." Here the magistrates interrogated, among others, the notorious "witches" Sarah Good, Tituba Indian, Martha Corey, and Rebecca Nurse. In 1701, a new meetinghouse was erected on the site of the current First Church and this meetinghouse abandoned. The Darling-Prince House (circa 1681), which now stands on the site, was moved here in the nineteenth century. It is privately owned.

4. First Church (corner of Hobart and Centre Streets). This is the present site of the First Church. In 1701, the old meetinghouse in which the witchcraft examinations took place was abandoned and a new meetinghouse erected on this spot. It was in this second meetinghouse that Ann Putnam, Jr. rose in her pew to ask forgiveness of those she had maligned in 1692. The present church building is modern.

5. Sarah Holten House (Plate 15; 171 Holten Street at the intersection of Holten and Centre Streets). In 1692, this house was the home of the widow Sarah Holten. Three years earlier, after Sarah's swine had uprooted Rebecca Nurse's garden, Rebecca had become so incensed that she stormed over

to the Holten house and upbraided Sarah's husband, Benjamin. "All we could say to hir could no ways passifie hir,"Sarah later testified, "but she continewed Railing and scolding agrat while." A short while later, Benjamin Holten fell ill "being much pained at his stomack and often struck blind . . . about a fortnight before he dyed he was taken with strange and violent fitts acting much like to our poor bewicthed parsons." The quotations are from Sarah's 1692 testimony that helped send Rebecca to the gallows. The Holten house is open to the public.

6. Rebecca Nurse House (Plate 14; 149 Pine Street, located near the intersection of Pine and Adams Streets). Built in 1678, this house was the home of Francis and Rebecca Nurse in 1692. In March of that year, Israel and Elizabeth Porter, friends of the Nurses, came here to tell Rebecca that she had been accused of witchcraft. They found the old woman, they wrote, in "A weak and Lowe condition in body as shee told us and had been sicke allmost A weak." Upon learning that she herself had been denounced, Rebecca "sate still awhille being as it wear Amazed: and then shee said well as to this thing I am Innocent as the child unborne." She was arrested and later tried on 29 June 1692. When the jury found her not guilty, her accusers fell into such affliction that Chief Justice William Stoughton imposed on the jury to reconsider its verdict. When the jurors returned from their second deliberation, they had changed the verdict to guilty. Although Rebecca obtained a reprieve from Governor Phips, it was withdrawn when her accusers renewed their outcries against her. She was hanged on Gallows Hill on July 19. Her body was brought secretly back to this farm and buried in an unmarked grave. A monument to her memory stands in the family cemetery located on the farm. The Nurse house is open to the public. There is an admission charge.

7. Danvers Historical Society Building (13 Page Street). The Danvers Historical Society has several objects pertinent to

the witchcraft including artifacts uncovered at the excavation of the Salem Village parsonage in 1970. The basement houses the Brehaut Witchcraft Collection, the largest collection of written works about the hysteria. The building is open to the public. There is an admission charge.

8. Sarah Osborne House (Plate 7; 272 Maple Street opposite Gorman Road). This house, constructed c. 1660, was the home of Sarah Osborne in 1692. Sarah Osborne, Sarah Good, and Tituba Indian were the first persons accused of witchcraft by the circle of girls. Osborne was examined on March 1 by John Hathorne and Jonathan Corwin at the Salem Village meetinghouse. She denied any meddling with the devil and stated that "shee was more like to be bewitched than that she was a witch." An entry in a Boston jailer's accounts reads "To the Keeping of Sarah Osbourn from the 7'th of March to the 10'th of May when she died." She never came to trial. Old and infirm, she succumbed to the harsh treatment she received in prison. As a woman of property in the Village, she had created a scandal by marrying her manservant, Alexander Osborne. In 1692, she was a prime candidate for witchhood. The house has been moved here from its original site. It is privately owned.

9. Wadsworth Cemetery (located on Summer Street, about one-tenth mile north of its intersection with Maple Street). Several persons connected with the hysteria are buried here.

   a. Elizabeth Parris, wife of Reverend Samuel Parris, is buried here beneath a stone carved in the style of the Boston stonecutter William Mumford (Plate 2). Elizabeth was mistress of the Salem Village parsonage in 1692 and died four years later, aged "About 48 Years." Her husband wrote her epitaph. It reads:

      Sleep precious Dust no Stranger now to Rest.
      Thou hast thy longed wish in Abrahams Brest.
      Farewell best Wife, choice Mother, Neighbour, Friend.
      Weel wail the less for hopes of Thee i th End.

      S P

b. The cemetery also contains the unmarked graves of two of George Burroughs's wives who died while he was minister in Salem Village. During the hysteria, their ghosts supposedly appeared to his accusers, claiming that he had murdered them and seeking vengeance.

10. Joseph Putnam House (Plate 34; southeast portion of cloverleaf intersection of Route 1 and Route 62). Joseph Putnam, youngest brother of the persecuting Thomas, lived in this house in 1692. Unlike his brother, Joseph was an early and outspoken opponent of the witch hunt. When the examinations began, he reportedly stormed over to Thomas Putnam's house and confronted Ann Putnam, Sr. "If you dare to touch with your foul lies anyone belonging to my household," he told her, "you shall answer for it." For months Joseph kept horses saddled at all times and armed his family to guarantee their escape in case they were ever accused. They never were. In 1718, Joseph's son Israel was born in this house. Israel became one of the most colorful generals of the American Revolution. The Putnam house is privately owned.

(Plate 34; Site 10) Joseph Putnam House, Danvers.

11. Putnam Cemetery (located off a small asphalt path which begins at the entrance road to the Massachusetts Department of Public Works on Route 62, just west of its intersection with Route 1). Beneath the earthen mound, located to the left just inside the entrance to the cemetery, are the unmarked graves of Thomas Putnam, his wife, Ann Putnam, Sr., and their daughter Ann. In 1692, the Putnams were one of the most powerful families in Salem Village. They played a major role in the witch hunt. Both twelve-year-old Ann and her mother belonged to the accusing circle. Ann, Sr. and Thomas died within two weeks of one another in 1699; young Ann died seventeen years later. In 1706, she publicly asked forgiveness from those she had accused for the calamity she had brought upon them through her accusations in 1692.

12. Bridget Bishop House (Plate 19; 238 Conant Street). In 1692, the condemned witch Bridget Bishop lived with her husband, Edward, in the old wing of this house. Arrested on April 18, she was examined the following day at Ingersoll's ordinary in Salem Village. "I am innocent to a Witch," she told the magistrates. "I know not what a Witch is." On June 2, she was tried and found guilty of witchcraft and was executed eight days later, the first of the nineteen persons hanged. Years earlier, her neighbors had complained to Reverend John Hale that she "did entertaine people in her house at unseasonable houres in the night to keep drinking and playing at shovel-board whereby . . . young people were in danger to bee corrupted." Bridget also owned a second house which stood in Salem. In the cellar walls of the Salem house, John Bly and his son William "found Severall popitts [dolls] made up of Raggs And hoggs Brusells w'th headles pins in Them." The Bishop house is privately owned.

Peabody

13. John Proctor House (Plate 16; on Lowell Street, one-tenth mile south of its intersection with Prospect Street). John Proctor, an early opponent of the witch hunt, lived in this

house in 1692. One of the afflicted girls, Mary Warren, was a maidservant in his household. Proctor had cured her fits with a good whipping and maintained that the others could be cured with similar treatment. In April 1692, John and his wife Elizabeth were accused of witchcraft. John was tried in early August and hanged later that month. Elizabeth was found pregnant at the time of her condemnation and was granted a stay of execution. She would escape the gallows and eventually remarry. The stream which runs behind the house is known to this day as Proctor Brook. The Proctor house is privately owned.

Salem

The county seat of Essex, Salem was the scene of the witchcraft trials in 1692. Those condemned were hanged on Gallows Hill. Giles Corey, who refused to stand trial, was pressed to death in a Salem field.

14. Site of the Courthouse in 1692 (Plate 25; marker on the wall of the Masonic Temple on Washington Street, about 100 feet south of the intersection of Washington and Lynde Streets). In 1692, the Salem courthouse stood in the middle of Washington Street just south of its present-day intersection with Lynde Street. It was here that all nineteen persons executed as witches were tried and condemned by the Court of Oyer and Terminer. The original edifice was torn down in 1760. The engraving on the frontispiece shows how this portion of Washington Street looked in the 1830s when a courthouse still stood in the middle of the street.

15. Site of the Meetinghouse of the First Church in Salem (Plate 17; marker located on Essex Street near the southeast corner of its intersection with Washington Street). In 1692, the meetinghouse of the First Church stood on this site. On April 11, Sarah Cloyce and John and Elizabeth Proctor were examined here. On the day of her trial, Bridget Bishop's specter reportedly pried up a plank from the meet-

inghouse and sent it crashing about the interior. Barely one month later, on July 3, Rebecca Nurse was brought here and publicly excommunicated.

16. Charter Street Cemetery (on Charter Street, between Lafayette and Liberty Streets). Here are buried four persons connected with the witchcraft.

a. Magistrate John Hathorne, who served as an interrogator in most of the witchcraft examinations and later as a member of the Court of Oyer and Terminer, died on 10 May 1717, aged seventy-six years. Hathorne's most famous descendant was the writer Nathaniel Hawthorne who added a "w" to the family name. Hawthorne wrote that his great-great-grandfather "inherited the persecuting spirit, and made himself so conspicuous in the martyrdom of the witches, that their blood may fairly be said to have left a stain upon him."

b. Bartholomew Gedney. A native of Salem and a physician by profession, Gedney was present at several of the examinations and later served as a member of the Court of Oyer and Terminer. He was present at the examination of his friend John Alden on 31 May 1692 in Salem Village. When Gedney saw how Alden tormented the girls, he told Alden that he had "always look'd upon him to be an honest Man, but now he did see cause to alter his judgment." Gedney is buried beneath a red sandstone table stone (Plate 22) located about sixty feet from the Charter Street entrance to the cemetery. The inscription on the table stone reads in part: "Here Lyes Interred ye Body of Colln Bartho Gedney Esqr. Aetat 57 Obt 28 Febr 1697."

c. "Mary Corry ye Wife of Giles Corry Aged 63 years Dyed August ye 27 1684" (Plate 12). This was Corey's second wife who died eight years before the hysteria. By 1692, Corey had remarried. Accused as a witch, he was pressed to death on September 19 for refusing to stand trial. His third wife, Martha, was hanged on Gallows Hill three days later. Both of their graves have been lost to history.

d. It is probable that Reverend Nicholas Noyes, minister of Salem during the witchcraft, lies buried here in an unmarked grave. Noyes was born in Newbury in 1647 and graduated from Harvard College in 1667. In May 1683, he became assistant minister in Reverend John Higginson's First Church in Salem. Noyes played an active role in the witchcraft prosecutions. At Martha Corey's examination in Salem Village on March 21, he remarked, "I believe it is apparent she practiseth Witchcraft in the congregation." When John Alden asserted during his examination in May that the afflicted girls accused innocent people, Noyes interrupted him "and so went on with Discourse, and stopt Aldin's mouth." Noyes later acknowledged his error and repented his treatment of those who had been accused of witchcraft. Tradition states that in 1717, he suffered an internal hemorrhage and died choking on his own blood, fulfilling Sarah Good's 1692 prophecy to him that "God will give you Blood to drink." Samuel Sewall later wrote that Noyes was "*Malleus Haereticorum*"—the "hammer of heretics."

17. Essex Institute (located on Essex Street, about one half block west of its intersection with Hawthorne Boulevard). The Essex Institute houses the bulk of the original documents pertaining to the accusations, examinations, trials, and executions of the witches. The collection also contains other mementoes of the hysteria, most notably the walking canes used by the arthritic George Jacobs, Sr. who was executed for witchcraft. The afflicted girls asserted that Jacobs's specter beat them with these canes. The Institute is open to the public. There is an admission charge.

18. Saint Peter's Church (located on the northeast corner of Brown and St. Peter Streets). This church was established

in 1733 largely through the support of the wealthy Salem merchant Philip English. English was accused of witchcraft in 1692 but escaped from prison and fled to New York. The sheriff, George Corwin, seized English's property for the Crown. When English returned to Salem in 1693, he found his home ransacked and his warehouses empty. After Corwin's death in 1697, English seized his corpse and forced Corwin's executors to pay him reparations for his losses in 1692. English is buried in an unmarked place beneath the church chapel which was built at a later date over the old Anglican cemetery. A small exhibit in his honor can be found inside.

19. Path to Gallows Hill. In 1692, the Salem jail stood on St. Peter Street (then called "Prison Lane") near its intersection with Federal Street. The traditional route taken by the condemned from the jail to Gallows Hill was through St. Peter Street, down Essex Street, and then through Boston Street to the point of its present intersection with Aborn Street, and from there to the summit of Gallows Hill. This roundabout path permitted the least precipitous approach to the brow of the hill.

20. Superior Court Building (red stone building on Federal Street near the northwest corner of its intersection with Washington Street). Several artifacts relevant to the witch hunt can be found in a small case in the office of the Clerk of Court. These include the 1692 seal of Essex County, used to legalize documents pertaining to the witchcraft, and several straight pins, admitted as evidence in the trials and said to have been used by the witches to prick their victims.

21. Jonathan Corwin House (Plate 8; located at the northwest corner of the intersection of Essex and North Streets). This house was probably built in the early 1670s and not in 1642. Jonathan Corwin, a Salem merchant, purchased the house from Nathaniel Davenport of Boston in 1675 and was living here in 1692. Corwin presided over many of the witch-

craft examinations and later served on the Court of Oyer and Terminer. There is a tradition that some of those accused of witchcraft were examined in the lower front room on the right as one faces the front of the house. Although the house is known locally as the "Witch House," no person accused of witchcraft either lived or was imprisoned here. The house is open to the public. There is an admission charge.

22. Broad Street Cemetery (located at the southeast corner of the intersection of Broad and Winthrop Streets). Beneath a small, white obelisk (Plate 9) lie the remains of George and Jonathan Corwin, together with other members of that extensive family. George, who was only twenty-five at the time of the hysteria, served as the high sheriff of Essex County in 1692. In this capacity he directed the confiscation of property from those convicted of witchcraft and carried out the death sentences of the nineteen who were hanged and of Giles Corey who was pressed to death for refusing to stand trial. George's funeral in 1697 was delayed by Philip English, who sought to recoup some of the fortune Corwin had seized from him in 1692 when English stood accused of witchcraft.

    Jonathan Corwin, a Salem merchant and the owner of the still-standing "Witch House," served as a magistrate at many of the examinations and later as a justice of the Court of Oyer and Terminer. He died on 9 June 1718, aged seventy-eight years.

23. Summit of Gallows Hill (Plate 26; intersection of Hanson and South Streets, best approached from Hanson Street). The Salem witchcraft authority, Charles W. Upham, chose this hill as the probable site of the hangings of the nineteen condemned witches in 1692. Executions for witchcraft occurred here on June 10, July 19, August 19, and September 22. After the September hangings, the Reverend Nicholas Noyes, turning to the eight bodies hanging from the tree, remarked, "What a sad thing it is to see Eight Firebrands of

Hell hanging there." The present author believes that the actual site of the executions lies on a lower hill nearer the town. The great height and rugged terrain of this hill would have precluded transporting the condemned to this site in a cart, which is known to have occurred.

Beverly

Several persons accused of witchcraft came from Beverly. Reverend John Hale, who lived in Beverly, was minister there in 1692.

24. John Hale House (Plate 3; 39 Hale Street). Hale built this house in 1694 and lived here until his death on 15 May 1700. A graduate of Harvard College in 1657, Hale became minister of the First Church in Beverly in 1665, a position he held for over thirty years. In 1692, he was one of the three North Shore ministers who ardently supported the witch hunt. When his own wife, Sarah, was accused he found reason to change his opinion. In this house in 1697 he wrote his brief history of the Salem tragedy entitled *A Modest Enquiry into the Nature of Witchcraft*. The house is open to the public. There is an admission charge.

25. Ancient Burial Ground (located between Hale Street and Abbott Street, behind the Central Fire Station). Reverend John Hale, minister in Beverly, is buried here in the Hale family plot (Plate 4). Beside him are buried two of his wives including Sarah, whom Mary Herrick accused of witchcraft. Sarah Hale died on 20 May 1697 at the age of forty-one.

26. Beverly Historical Society (located at 110 Cabot Street between Franklin Place and Central Street). The Beverly Historical Society collection contains two objects relevant to the witchcraft: a copy of the 1702 printing of John Hale's *A Modest Enquiry* and the halberd which was carried by the bailiff during the witchcraft trials and executions. The His-

torical Society is open to the public. There is an admission charge.

27. Ancient North Beverly Cemetery (located on a wooded spot on Conant Street, one-tenth mile east of its intersection with Cabot Street). Joseph Herrick, the constable in 1692, is buried here (Plate 13). Herrick arrested Tituba Indian, Sarah Osborne, and Martha Corey and brought them to their examinations in Salem Village. An entry in innkeeper Nathaniel Ingersoll's accounts reads "To Constable Herrick p̄ Drink & Cake . . . 6d." Herrick also gave testimony against Sarah Good who was later hanged. The inscription on Herrick's gravestone reads: "Here Lyes ye Body of Mr Joseph Herrick Who Died Febury ye 4th in ye 73 Year of His Age 1717/18."

Wenham

28. Old Wenham Burying Ground (located on Main Street (Route 1A) in Wenham, a short distance north of Wenham Lake). Here are buried several men of Wenham who played parts in the witchcraft hysteria.

   a. Joseph Gerrish, minister of the First Church of Wenham in 1692, is buried here beneath a red sandstone table stone (Plate 32). The inscription on his tomb reads: "Rev. Joseph Gerrish Born at Newbury Mar. 23, 1650 Graduated at Harvard College 1669 Ordained at Wenham Jan 12, 1674 Died in the Pastoral Office Jan 6, 1720." In 1692, four of Gerrish's parishioners were members of the jury which sat in judgment in Salem. In November 1692, Mary Herrick came to Gerrish complaining that Reverend John Hale's wife afflicted her. Her accusation caused Hale to oppose finally the witchcraft proceedings.

   b. "Here Lyes Buried the Body of Capt. Thomas Ffisk Who Decd Februry ye 5th 1723 in ye 70th Year of His Age. The Righteous shall be had in Everlasting Remembrance" (Plate 33). Fisk served as a member of the jury which convicted many of those condemned and executed for witchcraft in 1692. He was the son of the jury foreman, Thomas Fisk, Sr. Both men signed a public confession in 1697 stating that they "were sadly deluded and mistaken" in 1692.

c. "Here Lyeth ye body of Decn [Deacon] William Fisk who died Febry ye 5th 1727/8 Aged 85 years." William Fisk also served as a juror at the Salem trials in 1692 and later signed the 1697 confession of error.

29. Solart-Woodward House (Plate 6; 106 Main Street in Wenham, a short distance north of the Wenham Burying Ground). This house was built around 1670 and was the home of John Solart, Sr. who kept an inn here. His daughter Sarah, who was born 14 July 1653, later married William Good and moved away to Salem Village. Sarah Good was one of the first three persons accused of witchcraft in 1692 and was hanged on July 19. At her execution, she told Reverend Nicholas Noyes that "God will give you Blood to drink." The house is privately owned.

30. Claflin-Gerrish-Richards House (Plate 31; 132 Main Street, opposite its intersection with Monument Street). Reverend Joseph Gerrish lived here in 1692. It was here that Mary Herrick met with John Hale and Joseph Gerrish and told them that the specter of Hale's wife afflicted her. The house dates from the time period 1662–73 and is the office of the Wenham Historical Association. It is open to the public.

Marblehead

31. Redd's Pond (located at the intersection of Pond and Norman Streets). This pond was named for Wilmott Redd, a Marblehead woman accused of witchcraft and examined in Salem Village on 31 May 1692. At her examination, the afflicted girls cried that her specter tormented them and urged

them to sign the devil's book. When Susannah Sheldon, one of the afflicted girls, was ordered to approach Redd, she "was knock down before she came to her, & being so carryed to said Redd in a fit, was made well after said Redd had graspt her arm." Wilmott Redd was tried at the September 17 sitting of the Court of Oyer and Terminer and executed on September 22. Her house once stood in the vicinity of the pond "upon the hill by the meet'house."

32. Ambrose Gale House (Plate 30; 17 Franklin Street, between Washington and Selman Streets). Ambrose Gale lived here in 1692. Together with Charity Pitman and Sarah Doddy, he testified that Wilmott Redd had cursed a Mrs. Syms with an enduring case of constipation. The house was originally built around 1663 and is privately owned.

33. Old Burial Hill (off Orne Street, immediately adjacent to Redd's Pond). Ambrose Gale's wife Mary is buried here. Her epitaph reads: "Here Lyeth ye Body of Mary Galle ye Wife of Ambros Galle Aged 63 Years Decd February ye 5 1694/5." Of particular interest in this cemetery, though totally unrelated to the witchcraft, is the superb gravestone of Susanna Jayne, carved by the eighteenth-century master stonecutter Henry Christian Geyer.

North Andover

In 1692, North Andover was known simply as "Andover." It became embroiled in the witchcraft in July 1692 when Joseph Ballard brought several of the afflicted girls there to determine the cause of his wife's illness. Within several weeks, over fifty people were accused of witchcraft. Many of them confessed. The accusations in Andover abated after an unknown Boston man threatened to bring a slander suit against those who had accused him.

34. Old Burying Ground (on Academy Road, one-tenth mile from its intersection with Main Street in North Andover).

(Plate 35; Site 34c) Grave of William Barker, Sr., North Andover.

Some important figures in the Andover witch hunt are buried here.

a. Timothy Swan, who accused many of his neighbors in
   Andover of afflicting him, is buried here (Plate 28). His
   epitaph reads: "Timothy Swan Died February ye 2
   1692/3 & in ye 30 year of His Age." His is the only
   marked gravesite of an accuser known today.

      The peculiar notation of dates on these gravestones is
   worth mentioning. In the seventeenth century, England
   and her colonies officially began the New Year on March
   25. The last day of the year fell on March 24. Around
   1690, an impetus arose to adopt the Gregorian calendar
   and begin the New Year on January 1 instead of March

25. Consequently, dates in January, February, and early March during this time were often given fractional notations, such as 1692/3: still 1692 under the old calendar but under the new calendar already 1693. January 1 was not officially made the first day of the year in English North America until 1752.

b. Reverend Thomas Barnard, Andover's assistant minister in 1692, is buried here beneath a simple headstone (Plate 27). Barnard graduated from Harvard College in 1679 and came to Andover in 1682, joining Reverend Francis Dane. Barnard was present at the Andover meetinghouse during some of the examinations there. The accused were blindfolded, led before the afflicted girls, and made to touch them. It was presumptive proof of witchcraft if the witch's touch cured the girls' fits. The meetinghouse where these examinations took place stood on the triangular plot of land across from the cemetery at the intersection of Academy Road and Court Street. Barnard's epitaph reads: "Here Lyes Buried ye Body of ye Revernd Mr Thomas Barnard Who Departed this Life Octor 13th Anno Domi 1718 AEtatis Suae 62."

c. "Here Lyes Buried The Body of William Barker Who Died March The 4th 1718 In 73rd Year of His Age" (Plate 35). William Barker, Sr. was arrested and examined for witchcraft in Salem on 29 August 1692. He readily confessed to the charge. He told the magistrates that the witches' "design was to Destroy Salem Village, and to begin at the Ministers House, and to destroy the Church of God, and to set up Satans Kingdom, and then all will be well." Despite his confession, Barker survived the hysteria.

d. William Barker, Jr., who was only fourteen at the time of the hysteria, is also buried here. He was examined on 1 September 1692 and, like his father, confessed. He had so recently converted to witchcraft, he told the magistrates, that he had "not been in the snare of the Devil above six Dayes." Young Barker was released on bail in January 1693 and was tried the following May in Ipswich. He was acquitted. His epitaph reads: "Here Lies Buried the Body of Mr William Barker Who Died Janry 16 1745 In 67 Year Of His Age."

Haverhill

35. Pentucket Cemetery (located at the intersection of Water and Mill Streets). In this cemetery, beneath a white obelisk (Plate 23), is buried Major Nathaniel Saltonstall, a member of the Court of Oyer and Terminer. After resigning from the court in June 1692, Saltonstall became a prominent critic of the Salem proceedings and was himself accused of witchcraft. Following his graduation from Harvard College in 1659, Saltonstall had embarked on a military career. A contemporary described him as among "the most popular and principled military men" in the colony. In 1697, Saltonstall commanded the Haverhill defenses. When the town was destroyed in an Indian raid, he was censured by the colony for negligent behavior. He died in Haverhill on 21 May 1707 "after a half years Consumptive illness."

Amesbury

36. Site of Susannah Martin's House (Plate 20; marker located at the end of Martin Street, which intersects with Route 110 at the Red Pepper Restaurant about one-half mile west of the intersection of Routes 110 and 150). Susannah Martin's house stood on this site in 1692. She was examined in Salem Village on May 2, tried for witchcraft on June 29, and hanged on Gallows Hill on July 19. Cotton Mather called her "one of the most Impudent, Scurrilous, wicked creatures in the world." The marker in Amesbury, however, claims that she was "an honest, hard working Christian woman."

(Plate 36; Site 37)
Grave of Major
Robert Pike,
Salisbury.

Salisbury

37. Old Burying Ground (on Route 1A, two-tenths of a mile east of its intersection with Route 110). Here is buried Major Robert Pike (Plate 36) who lived in Salisbury and was an assistant of the colony. Pike recorded much of the testimony given against Susannah Martin after her arrest in May 1692. In August, however, he wrote a forceful letter to Jonathan Corwin in which he attacked spectral evidence. As long as spectral evidence was admissible in court, he wrote, "the Devil is accuser and witness." Pike signed an affidavit in defense of Mary Bradbury of Salisbury who was convicted of witchcraft on September 9 but escaped hanging. He died in 1706 at the age of ninety.

Boston

Several of the most prominent actors in the witchcraft proceedings, including five members of the Court of Oyer and Terminer, were from Boston or its immediate vicinity.

38. King's Chapel Burial Ground (located at the intersection of Tremont and School Streets). Two people connected with the witchcraft are buried here.

   a. Major General Wait Still Winthrop, a grandson of Massachusetts's first governor, John Winthrop, is buried in the Winthrop tomb (Plate 24). Wait Still served Massachusetts as a member of the council and as commander-in-chief of the provincial forces. In 1692, he sat on the Court of Oyer and Terminer and later on the Superior Court which tried the remaining witchcraft cases in 1693. He died in 1717 at the age of seventy-five.

   b. Thomas Brattle, one of the most outspoken opponents of the witchcraft, is buried beneath a black table stone with a brick foundation in the northeast portion of the cemetery (Plate 29). The inscription on the stone can barely be discerned. It reads:

   > HERE LYES THE BODY OF THOMAS
   > BRATTLE ESQR ONE OF HER MAJESTYES
   > JUSTICES FOR THE COUNTY OF SUFFOLK
   > & TREASURER OF HARVARD COLLEGE WHO
   > DYED MAY THE 18th 1713 ANNO AETATIS 55.

   Brattle graduated from Harvard College in 1676 and later became a fellow of London's Royal Society. In October 1692, he wrote his famous "Letter" which denounced the witch trials and helped bring them to a close. It is widely believed that Brattle supplied much of the material contained in Robert Calef's *More Wonders of the Invisible World*.

   c. On the inside walls of the King's Chapel building can be found a monument to Thomas Newton, who served as King's Attorney and prosecuted the witchcraft cases until 26 July 1692. On that day he was succeeded by Anthony Checkley, the colony's attorney general. Newton had come to Massachusetts from England in 1688 and was one of the first legally trained lawyers in Massachusetts. Capital cases must have been his specialty. In 1691, he served as attorney general for New York where he successfully prosecuted several cases of high treason. Checkley, on the other hand, was a merchant by vocation and lacked any legal training. Governor Phips reprieved three persons condemned in January 1693 after Checkley informed him "that there was the same reason to clear the three condemned as the rest according to his Judgment." Phips's action so enraged Chief Justice William Stoughton that he temporarily refused to participate in the trials. Both Newton and Checkley died in Boston, Newton in 1721 and Checkley in 1708.

39. Granary Burying Ground (located on Tremont Street, beside the Park Street Church). Samuel Sewall, a justice on the Court of Oyer and Terminer, is buried beneath a red sandstone table stone in the northwest portion of the cemetery (Plate 18). The stone's surface is inscribed: "Honl. Judge Sewall's Tomb Now the property of his Heirs Philip R. Ridgway 1810 Ralph Huntington 1812 No. 185 Ralph Huntington." Born in England in 1652, Sewall attended Harvard College and afterward served in the militia where he was commissioned a captain. His marriage in 1676 brought him great wealth and established him as one of the most prominent men in the colony. He is best known for the diary of his life which he kept for many years. Historians have used his diary to obtain glimpses into daily life in seventeenth-century Massachusetts. One of his diary entries in November 1685 records that Reverend George Burroughs dined at Sewall's house in Boston. Seven years later, Sewall would sit on the court which would condemn Burroughs to death. Sewall was the lone court member to ask forgiveness publicly for his part in the Salem tragedy.

40. Copp's Hill Burying Ground (located at the intersection of Hull and Snowhill Streets). Mather tomb: beneath a simple table stone (Plate 5) are buried three ministers of the powerful Mather family: Increase, Cotton, and Samuel—father,

son, and grandson, respectively. The original inscription on the stone reads:

> THE REVEREND DOCTORS
> INCREASE, COTTON,
> & SAMUEL MATHER
> were intered in this Vault.
> 'Tis the Tomb of our Father's
> MATHER—CROCKER'S
> I DIED Augt 27th 1723 AE 84
> C DIED FEB 13th 1727 AE 65
> S DIED June 27th 1785 AE 79

a. Increase Mather: born in 1639, he was named Increase, his son later wrote, "because of the never-to-be-forgotten *Increase*, of every sort, wherewith GOD favoured the Country, about the time of his Nativity." Increase graduated from Harvard College in 1656 and went to England shortly afterward, but was compelled to return to Massachusetts in 1661 at the restoration of Charles II. He became minister of the North Church in Boston, and in 1685 was appointed to the presidency of Harvard, a position which he held until 1701. Between 1688 and 1692, Increase lived in England and renegotiated the new Massachusetts charter. He returned to Massachusetts in May 1692 with the charter and the new royal governor, Sir William Phips, only to find the colony besieged by witches. Although critical of the witchcraft proceedings, Increase was present at George Burroughs's trial and felt him justly condemned. In October 1692, his address to a convocation of ministers, later published under the title *Cases of Conscience Concerning Evil Spirits Personating Men*, helped turn the tide against spectral evidence. When Robert Calef's reappraisal of the Salem witchcraft, *More Wonders of the Invisible World*, was published in 1700, Increase was so incensed by its treatment of him and his son Cotton that he had the book publicly burned in the college yard.

b. Cotton Mather: born in 1663, Cotton Mather was named for his maternal grandfather, John Cotton. After graduating from Harvard College in 1678, he became assistant minister of his father's North Church. He had relatively indirect dealings with the Salem witchcraft: authoring the ministers' advice to the court in June, attending the August hangings at which he addressed the crowd following George Burroughs's execution, and writing a brief account of the Salem trials entitled *Wonders of the Invisible World*. The last of these, however, linked his name irretrievably with the witchcraft. His treatment of the condemned witches was so unfeeling and slanted that it helped prompt Robert Calef to write *More Wonders of the Invisible World*, which dealt Mather's reputation a blow from which it never recovered. The one worldly honor Cotton coveted, the Harvard presidency, was denied him in part because of Calef's writings. Cotton died in 1727, only four years after his beloved father.

41. Old Burying Ground, Dorchester (located at the intersection of Stoughton Street and Columbia Road in Dorchester). In this ancient cemetery, beneath an imposing marble table stone adorned with skulls (Plate 21), lies buried William Stoughton, the chief justice of the Court of Oyer and Terminer. Stoughton was born in 1631 and graduated from Harvard College in 1650. He then went to England to continue his education and received the degree of Master of Arts from Oxford. In 1662, following the restoration of Charles II, he returned to Massachusetts where he refused a church calling and served on the Massachusetts courts. In 1692, he was appointed lieutenant governor under the new charter. When the Court of Oyer and Terminer was appointed, Governor Phips chose Stoughton to serve as its chief justice, in which capacity he proved the scourge of the accused witches. In 1694, when Phips returned to England, Stoughton served as acting-governor in his stead until 1698. He served as chief justice of the Massachusetts courts until shortly before his death in 1701.

(Plate 37; Site 42) Grave of Robert Calef, Roxbury.

His original tombstone no longer marks his grave but has been replaced by a more modern version. The original epitaph, which was written in Latin and was not placed on this latest stone, read in part:

> Whom have we lost—
>   STOUGHTON!
>   Alas!
> I have said sufficient, Tears press,
>   I keep silence.
>   He lived Seventy Years;
> On the Seventh of July, in the Year of Safety
>   1701,
>   He died.
> Alas! Alas! What Grief!

Indeed, history remembers all too well "What Grief" he brought to those accused in 1692.

42. Eustis Street Burying Ground, Roxbury (located at the intersection of Eustis and Washington Streets in Roxbury). Robert Calef, author of *More Wonders of the Invisible World*, is buried here beneath a small gravestone (Plate 37) carved by a member of the Foster family of Dorchester. The inscription reads: "Here lyes Buried the Body of Mr. Robert Calef Aged Seventy one years Died April The Thirteenth 1719." Calef wrote his *More Wonders*, he tells us, as a rebuke to those who still believed in the methods used in the 1692 witch hunt. He feared the witch hunt "should be Acted over again inforced by their Example, rather than that it should Remain as a Warning to Posterity." It is widely believed that Calef received much of his material for the book from Thomas Brattle. The book's attacks on Reverend Cotton Mather were so harsh that no Boston printer would accept it, so Calef was forced to send it to England for publication. Calef himself was a cloth merchant and served Roxbury as a selectman until his death.

Maps

This section includes detailed maps of Danvers, Salem, and Beverly, and a less-detailed general map of Essex County. Detailed maps for the other towns listed in the guide's sites section have been omitted, since few sites are located in these towns. These sites, however, can easily be found using the addresses given in the sites section.

Sites in Danvers, Salem, and Beverly are located on the maps by numbers which correspond to the numbers in the sites section.

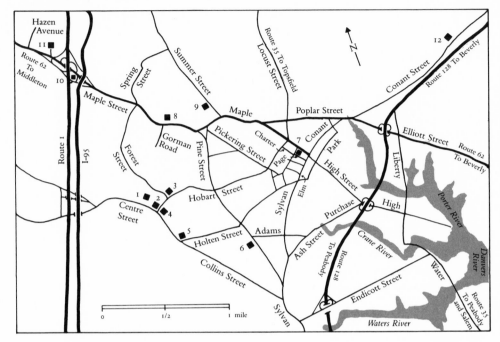

Danvers

1. Foundations of the 1692 Parsonage.
2. Nathaniel Ingersoll's Ordinary.
3. Site of the Salem Village Meetinghouse.
4. First Church.
5. Sarah Holten House.
6. Rebecca Nurse House.
7. Danvers Historical Society Building.
8. Osborne House.
9. Wadsworth Cemetery.
10. Joseph Putnam House.
11. Putnam Cemetery.
12. Bridget Bishop House.

14. Site of the Courthouse in 1692.
15. Site of the Meetinghouse of the First Church in Salem.
16. Charter Street Cemetery.
17. Essex Institute.
18. Saint Peter's Church.
20. Superior Court Building.
21. Jonathan Corwin House.
22. Broad Street Cemetery.
23. Summit of Gallows Hill.

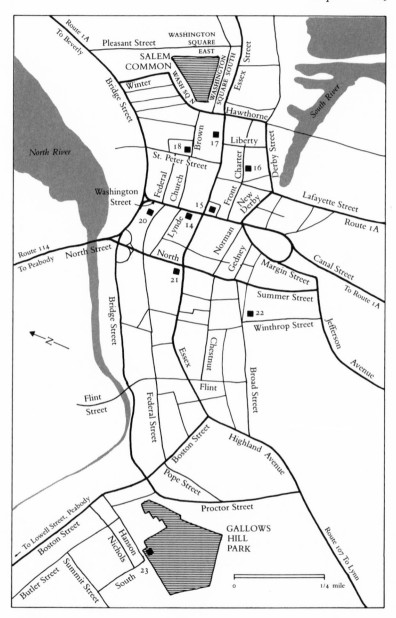

Salem

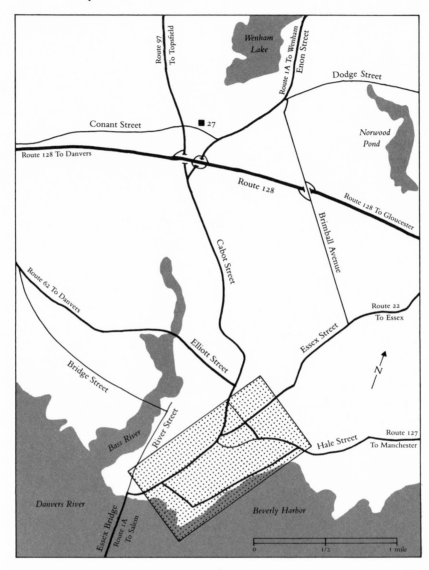

Wenham
Lake

Route 97
To Topsfield

Route 1A To Wenham

Enon Street

Dodge Street

Norwood
Pond

Conant Street

■ 27

Route 128 To Danvers

Route 128

Route 128 To Gloucester

Cabot Street

Brimball Avenue

Route 62 To Danvers

Route 22
To Essex

Elliott Street

Essex Street

Bridge Street

River Street

Hale Street

Route 127
To Manchester

Bass River

Danvers River

Essex Bridge

Route 1A
To Salem

Beverly Harbor

N

0   1/2   1 mile

Beverly

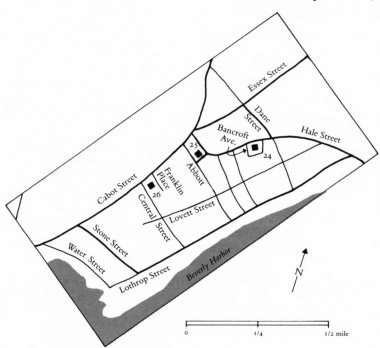

24. John Hale House.
25. Ancient Burial Ground.
26. Beverly Historical Society.
27. Ancient North Beverly
    Cemetery.

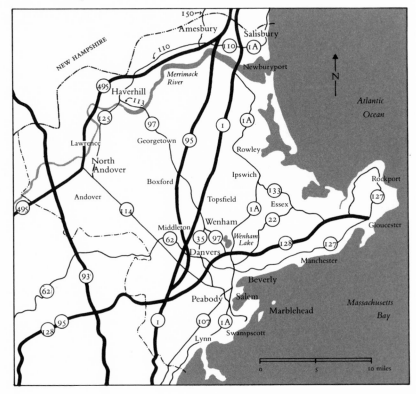

Essex County

Selected Bibliography

Primary Sources

Boyer, Paul, and Nissenbaum, Stephen, eds. *The Salem Witchcraft Papers: Verbatim Transcripts of the Legal Documents of the Salem Witchcraft Outbreak of 1692.* 3 vols. New York: Da Capo Press, 1977.

This three volume work contains transcripts of most of the known legal documents pertaining to the Salem witchcraft trials. An invaluable source for anyone interested in what happened in Salem in 1692.

Boyer, Paul, and Nissenbaum, Stephen, eds. *Salem-Village Witchcraft: A Documentary Record of Local Conflict in Colonial New England.* Belmont, Calif.: Wadsworth Publishing Company, 1972.

Primarily a collection of documents concerning the factional disputes that wracked Salem Village in the fifteen years preceding 1692. The editors do not attempt much historical analysis in this book but reserve it for their later work, *Salem Possessed* (see below).

Burr, George L., ed. *Narratives of the Witchcraft Cases: 1648–1706.* New York: Charles Scribner's Sons, 1914; reprint ed., New York: Barnes and Noble, 1975.

This work contains the important eyewitness accounts of the witchcraft: Deodat Lawson's *A Brief and True Narrative,* Thomas Brattle's "Letter," Governor Phips's letters to the Privy Council, Cotton Mather's *Wonders of the Invisible World,* Robert Calef's *More Wonders,* and John Hale's *A Modest Enquiry into the Nature of Witchcraft.* Traces the rise and fall of the witchcraft delusion as viewed by its contemporaries. The editor's footnotes are particularly enlightening; but the book's format does not provide a good chronological overview of the witchcraft events.

Drake, Samuel G., ed. *The Witchcraft Delusion in New England.* 3 vols. Roxbury, Mass.: W. Elliot Woodward, 1866; reprint ed., New York: Burt Franklin, 1970.

> A complete reprinting of Cotton Mather's *Wonders of the Invisible World* and Robert Calef's *More Wonders of the Invisible World,* containing material omitted by Burr. Drake's edition, with its copious footnotes, is considered the best-edited version of Mather's and Calef's books.

Hale, John. *A Modest Enquiry into the Nature of Witchcraft.* Boston: 1702; facsimile reproduction, Bainbridge, New York: York Mail-Print, 1973.

> Facsimile reproduction of Hale's work, printed in its entirety. When Hale's account was excerpted in Burr's *Narratives,* some very interesting and important material was omitted.

Secondary Sources

Boyer, Paul, and Nissenbaum, Stephen. *Salem Possessed: The Social Origins of Witchcraft.* Cambridge, Mass.: Harvard University Press, 1974.

> Posits that the social conflicts in Salem Village and the 1692 witch hunt resulted from deeply rooted tensions between an agrarian-based faction of farmers and the adherents to the emerging system of mercantile trade. Although this theory may explain one of the motive forces behind the Salem trials, it does not explain how the phenomenon came to engulf Essex County and to threaten the very foundation of Massachusetts Bay.

Demos, John P. *Entertaining Satan: Witchcraft and the Culture of Early New England.* Oxford: Oxford University Press, 1982.

> A landmark study of the psychological and social significance of witchcraft prosecutions in seventeenth-century New England. Demos examines in detail the "witches," their victims, and the social utility of witchcraft accusations. The Salem trials are for the most part omitted, however. Demos concludes that witchcraft accusations provided a means of control over deviant behavior and were abandoned when people no longer knew their neighbors so intimately or viewed them as possible sources of malefic harm.

Hansen, Chadwick. *Witchcraft at Salem.* New York: George Braziller, 1969.

> On the whole, Hansen's book is the best study of the Salem trials in this century. His emphasizing the reality of malefic witchcraft to

the seventeenth-century mind and his removing the stigma on Cotton Mather for his having "got up Salem witchcraft" are especially noteworthy. Hansen's failure to distinguish adequately between witchcraft and magic, however, leads him to the dubious conclusion that some of those executed in 1692 were, in fact, witches.

Hutchinson, Thomas. *The History of the Colony and Province of Massa-chusetts-Bay.* 3 vols. Edited by L.S. Mayo. Cambridge, Mass.: Harvard University Press, 1936.

Hutchinson's account of the Salem episode (vol. 2, pp. 9–47) is the first major account of the witch hunt not written by a contemporary. Contains transcripts of many documents pertinent to the Salem trials, the originals of which have since disappeared.

Kittredge, George Lyman. *Witchcraft in Old and New England.* Cambridge, Mass.: Harvard University Press, 1929.

One of the best books ever written about witchcraft in England and New England by an author with encyclopedic knowledge of the history of witchcraft. Kittredge maintains with considerable authority that the accession of James I to the English throne in 1603 did not cause the witchcraft prosecutions in seventeenth-century England. Chapter eighteen deals with witchcraft in New England.

Nevins, Winfield S. *Witchcraft in Salem Village in 1692.* Boston: Lea and Shepard, 1892.

A good older account of the Salem trials.

Starkey, Marion L. *The Devil in Massachusetts: A Modern Inquiry into the Salem Witch Trials.* New York: Alfred A. Knopf, 1950.

Starkey's book, although highly readable, is for the most part a reworking of Upham with a bit of modern psychology mixed in. As a reappraisal of the Salem trials, her book is unimportant.

Taylor, John M. *The Witchcraft Delusion in Colonial Connecticut, 1647–1697.* New York: The Grafton Press, 1908.

Taylor's book contains transcripts of numerous documents relating to the history of witchcraft in Connecticut, but it has little material pertinent to the Salem witch hunt. It does, however, include documents about witchcraft prosecutions in Fairfield, Connecticut in 1692 that took place in the wake of the Salem trials.

Upham, Charles W. *Salem Witchcraft.* 2 vols. Boston: Wiggins and Lunt, 1867; reprint ed., New York: Frederick Ungar, 1978.

The first major historical study of the Salem witchcraft, unfortunately written by a person with anti-Puritan sentiments. Upham's work is poorly documented and is replete with anti-Puritan bombast; but it nevertheless is a noteworthy achievement. Volume one presents a history of Salem Village prior to 1692. The second volume examines the witch hunt.

New England Funerary Art

Forbes, Harriette M. *Gravestones of Early New England and the Men Who Made Them.* Boston: Houghton Mifflin, 1927; reprint ed., New York: Da Capo Press, 1967.

The pioneering study of Puritan funerary art in colonial New England. Forbes's book examines the significance and symbolism of Puritan gravestone art and discusses the artists who created the American Puritans' finest achievement in the decorative arts.

Ludwig, Allan I. *Graven Images: New England Stonecarving and its Symbols, 1650–1815.* Middletown, Conn.: Wesleyan University Press, 1966.

An important scholarly work on the subject.

This book is set in Mergenthaler 202 Bembo. Paper is Mohawk Vellum seventy-pound cream white text. Binding material is Strathmore Pastelle Natural White eighty-pound cover.

Composition by G&S Typesetters, Austin, Texas. Printing and binding by Mercantile Printing Company, Worcester, Massachusetts. Designed by Dariel Mayer.